Anna Karenina

LEO TOLSTOY

Translated by Rosemary Edmonds

Level 6

Retold by Anne Collins
Series Editors: Andy Hopkins and Jocelyn Potter

T0385965

Pearson Education Limited

Edinburgh Gate, Harlow,

Essex CM20 2JE, England

and Associated Companies throughout the world.

ISBN: 978-1-4058-6529-6

This translation first published in Penguin Classics 1954

First published by Penguin Books 2001

This edition first published 2008

11

Original translation copyright © 1954 Rosemary Edmonds

Text copyright © Penguin Books Ltd 2001

This edition copyright © Pearson Education Ltd 2008

Typeset by Graphicraft Ltd, Hong Kong

Set in 11/14pt Bembo

Printed in China

SWTC/11

Published by Pearson Education Ltd

Every effort has been made to trace the copyright holders and we apologise in advance
for any unintentional omissions. We would be pleased to insert the appropriate
acknowledgement in any subsequent edition of this publication.

For a complete list of the titles available in the Pearson English Readers series, please
visit www.pearsonenglishreaders.com. Alternatively, write to your local Pearson Education
office or to Pearson English Readers Marketing Department, Pearson Education,
Edinburgh Gate, Harlow, Essex CM20 2JE, England.

Contents

Introduction

'Possibly I have made a mistake,' Karenin added.

'No,' said Anna slowly, looking with despair into his cold face. 'You have not made a mistake. I am listening to you, but I am thinking of him. I love him and I am his mistress. I hate you, I am afraid of you . . . You can do what you like with me.'

Anna Karenina is young, beautiful and full of life. She is the jewel of Petersburg society and is admired by everybody. Her husband is a respected but dull government official who is much older than she is. Deep inside Anna there is a secret emptiness that not even she knows about. Her only real love is for her son, but is that enough to keep her happy?

One day, her brother calls her from Moscow. His marriage is in serious trouble and he urgently needs his sister's help to persuade his wife not to leave him. Anna, with her easy nature and gentle charms, soon achieves her aim but, while in Moscow, she meets a handsome young man called Vronsky. A fire is lit in the shadowy depths of her heart. Excited by the heat of passion, but eaten by its flames, Anna is desperately torn between her love for Vronsky and her love for her son. Unable to lie to the people around her, she tells her husband the truth, and one of the greatest love stories in world literature tragically unfolds.

Anna Karenina, by Count Leo Nikolayevich Tolstoy (1828– 1910) has been called the greatest novel of all time. It covers an enormous range and depth of emotions – love, hate, despair, anger, pity, sorrow and joy – all set against the background of high society in late nineteenth-century Russia. The story took Tolstoy four years to write, from 1873 to 1877, and appeared part by part in a monthly magazine called the *Russian Messenger*.

However, the last part was not published in the magazine because the editor did not agree with the views expressed in the final scenes. The novel's first complete appearance, therefore, was in book form in 1878.

Tolstoy had first thought of calling his novel *Two Couples* or *Two Marriages*. Apart from the relationship between Anna and Vronsky, we also see the development of the relationship between Kitty and Levin, a quiet, shy, thoughtful man who prefers the peace and quiet of country life to the colourful but basically meaningless life of big city high society.

On one level, *Anna Karenina* can be read as a brilliantly-told story of tragic romance. In fact, many people criticized it when it was first published for exactly this reason. One writer called it, 'an unimportant romance of high life'. However, when we consider that Tolstoy himself (like Levin in the story), deeply disliked the extreme wealth and mindless behaviour of upper-class Russians at the time, we can also see the story at a deeper level: the difficulty of being truly honest when the rest of society only accepts falseness.

When Tolstoy first started *Anna Karenina*, he did not like his heroine very much, and did not even make her beautiful. But as the work progressed, his attitude towards her changed dramatically and he wrote of her with sympathetic admiration. The result is a complex character who is constantly at war with her own feelings. Anna can neither be completely honest nor completely false and it is this confusion which makes her, like Shakespeare's Hamlet, one of literature's most interesting creations.

Fyodor Dostoyevsky, the great Russian writer who wrote *Crime and Punishment*, was more accurate in his judgement on the book than most other commentators at the time. He described it as 'a perfect work of art'. Another important admirer of the book was the important twentieth-century Russian writer Vladimir Nabokov. He especially admired 'the perfect magic of

Tolstoy's style' and the way that Tolstoy used trains as a symbol of approaching tragedy throughout the book.

The story also, as we have seen, describes the very different kind of love story between Kitty and Levin. The joyous, honest and basically stable relationship between Levin and Kitty is in sharp contrast to the passionate but dark, unstable relationship between Anna and Vronsky. In the story, Levin represents Tolstoy himself. Tolstoy gives Levin the events of his own life and his own thoughts and ideas. The relationship between Levin and Kitty is mirrored in the relationship between Tolstoy and his wife, Sonya. Sonya used to joke to her husband about Levin, on one occasion saying, 'You are Levin plus talent, and Levin is an unbearable fellow!' Tolstoy, like Levin, found great comfort in his wife, with whom he lived very happily on his country estate, fathering thirteen children in fifteen years.

Tolstoy considered this book to be his first true novel. He did not consider his earlier book, *War and Peace* (1865–69) to be a real novel, because in it fiction was mixed with historical fact, and real people like Napoleon appeared. On 11 May 1873, he wrote to his friend Strakhov about his new work: 'I am writing a novel that has nothing to do with Peter the Great . . . This novel – I mean a novel, the first in my life – is very close to my heart, and I am completely wrapped up in it.'

Tolstoy had long had the idea for a novel about a beautiful society woman who has a relationship outside marriage. But a particular incident in 1872 caused him to write *Anna Karenina*. A young woman who had been rejected by her lover threw herself under a train at his local station. Tolstoy was deeply affected by seeing the body of this woman who, crazy with grief and jealousy, had given everything for love, even her life.

A short time later, in March 1873, Tolstoy picked up one of his children's books, a story by Pushkin, and read the first line aloud to Sonya, 'The guests arrived at the country house.' He turned to his wife and said, 'That's the way to begin,' meaning that a novel should begin the middle of the action, without long descriptions. That evening he wrote the first lines of *Anna Karenina*.

Today, the story still captures our imagination, and several film and TV adaptations have been made of it. The most famous film of the story, perhaps, is the 1935 Hollywood version directed by Clarence Brown, with Greta Garbo as Anna. Interestingly, in this film the relationship between Anna and Vronsky is shown to be completely immoral and wrong, and there is no mention at all of their child. The character of Karenin, Anna's husband, is pictured in a very sympathetic light. Tolstoy would not have approved!

Leo Tolstoy was born on 28 August 1828, the fourth of five children. His father was Count Nicholas Ilich Tolstoy and his mother was Princess Nikolayevna Volkonsky. His mother died in 1830, after giving birth to her fifth child. She was a very creative person, and a great story-teller, who was passionately interested in the development of her children and wanted them to grow up into men of ability. Tolstoy studied law and eastern languages at Kazan University, but left without a degree, dissatisfied with the quality of education at the university. In 1851, with large debts as a result of heavy betting, he joined the army with his elder brother, Nikolai. He also began his literary career, publishing three books about his life: *Childhood* (1852), *Boyhood* (1854) and *Youth* (1857).

One of his earliest published stories, *The Raid* (1852), was based on a true military adventure that his brother took part in. Tolstoy was already beginning his life-long hatred of war. 'Can it be,' he wrote, 'that there is not room for all men on this beautiful earth?' Fifty years later, Tolstoy returned to this period in his life with the short novel *Hadji Murad* (1904), which is still an extremely useful introduction to the background of Russia's present-day problems with Chechnya.

During the Crimean War, Tolstoy was a field gun commander and witnessed the famous battle for the town of Sebastopol (1854–55). After travelling around Europe in 1857, he settled in Yasnaya Polyana, where he started a school for peasant children. Believing that the secret of changing the world lay in education, he published magazines and text books on the subject of educational theory. In 1862, he married Sonya Andreyevna Behrs (1844–1919).

Tolstoy's fiction developed originally out of his diaries, in which he tried to understand his own feelings and actions in order to control them. *War and Peace* reflects Tolstoy's view that everything that happens in life is governed by a great universal plan, but we cannot live unless we believe that we have freedom of will. This idea occurs again in his other great novel, *Anna Karenina*, in which Anna struggles to find freedom in passionate love, but is powerless to control the events that result from her actions and which eventually destroy her.

After *Anna Karenina*, Tolstoy began to see himself more as a philosopher and a moral leader than an artist. In the 1880s, he wrote philosophical works such as *A Confession and What I Believe*. In 1884, he gave his estate to his family and tried to live as a wandering peasant. He wrote one more important novel, *Resurrection* (1899). He died in 1910 of a serious illness at a small railway station a long way from home. Eight years after his death, his wife was heard to say, 'I lived with Lev Nikolayevich for forty-eight years, but I never really learnt what kind of man he was.'

Tolstoy's ideas and teaching had a great influence on people in the twentieth century, including the Indian spiritual leader Gandhi. But his name will always be remembered as the writer of *War and Peace* and *Anna Karenina*.

Chapter 1   Affairs of the Heart

All happy families are alike, but an unhappy family is unhappy in its own way.

Everything had gone wrong in the Oblonsky household. The wife, Dolly, had found out that her husband had been having an affair with the children's French teacher, and had announced that she could not go on living in the same house. She did not leave her room, and her husband stayed away from home all day. Their five children wandered all over the house, not knowing what to do with themselves. The servants were quarrelling with each other, and the head cook had left.

On the third morning after the quarrel, Prince Stepan Oblonsky – Stiva, as he was generally called by his friends – awoke at his usual time of about eight o'clock. Suddenly he remembered why he was not in his usual bedroom but on a leather sofa in his study.

'Dolly will never forgive me – she cannot forgive me!' he thought. 'What have I done? It's all my fault! But I can't really be blamed. That's the whole tragedy.'

He remembered how he had come back from the theatre three nights ago, feeling very happy, and had found Dolly waiting for him in the bedroom with a note in her hand and an expression of horror, despair and anger on her face.

'What's this? What does it mean?' she had demanded coldly, holding out the note.

Oblonsky was so surprised that Dolly had discovered his affair that he had not known what to say. He had not tried to defend himself or to ask for forgiveness. He had only smiled his usual kind and rather foolish smile. Dolly had run from the room with a stream of angry and bitter words, and since then she had refused to see him.

'Why did I smile in that silly way?' thought Oblonsky. 'And what can I do now?' he asked himself again.

The affair with the French teacher was not the first affair that Oblonsky had had. He was not really sorry about it; he only regretted that he had not managed to hide things better from his wife. He was thirty-four years old, handsome and charming, but he was no longer in love with Dolly. She was a good wife and mother, but her youth and beauty had faded.

He rang the bell, and immediately a servant came in, carrying his boots, clothes and a telegram. Oblonsky tore open the telegram and read it, and his face brightened. It was from his sister, Anna, in Petersburg, where she lived with her husband and eight-year-old son. Dolly was very fond of Anna, and Oblonsky had written to her hoping that she might come and put things right between them. The telegram said Anna would be arriving in Moscow the next day.

When the servant had left the room, Oblonsky dressed with his usual care. Then he smoked a cigarette before crossing the room and opening the door into his wife's bedroom.

Dolly was standing in front of a cupboard, trying to make a decision. Her own things and the children's clothes lay everywhere on the floor. She was thinking that she ought to leave Oblonsky and take the children to her mother's. But in her heart she knew this was impossible because, in spite of everything, Oblonsky was her husband and she still loved him.

When she saw her husband come in, she felt even more annoyed. He looked so fresh and healthy, as if nothing in the world was wrong. Dolly pretended not to notice him, trying to appear strong and determined but only succeeding in looking lost and miserable.

'Anna is coming tomorrow,' said Oblonsky in a soft voice.

'Well, I can't receive her,' cried Dolly. 'I'm leaving you and going to my mother's.'

'Dolly, you must try and understand, you must see . . . '

'Go away, go away, go away!' Dolly cried without looking at him, as if the cry was torn from her body.

When Oblonsky saw Dolly's suffering face and heard the terrible despair in her voice, his eyes filled with tears.

'Dolly, please forgive me! Please think of the children – they've done nothing wrong. I'm the guilty one. Punish me for my sin! Tell me what to do – but, please, Dolly, forgive me!'

Dolly sat down and said, 'I *am* thinking of the children, Stiva, and I would do anything in the world for them. But I don't know what is best for them – whether I should take them away or leave them with a father who is immoral. How can we live together after what's happened? I hate you! You never loved me!' She rose quickly and moved towards the door.

'Dolly, one more word,' said Oblonsky, going after her.

'Go away!' she screamed. She went out, banging the door.

Oblonsky called his servant and told him to prepare a room for Anna. Then he put on his coat and went to his office.

Oblonsky had a well-paid position as head of one of Moscow's courthouses. He needed a job with a good salary because he always had a lot of debts. He had obtained this job through his sister Anna's husband, Alexei Karenin, who had an important position in the ministry to which the courthouse was attached.

Oblonsky was not hard-working, but he was clever, good-natured, charming and popular. People were always delighted to see him because he made them feel happy. 'Ah! Stiva! Oblonsky!' they would say with a smile of pleasure.

On arrival at the courthouse, Oblonsky went straight into a meeting to discuss a report. It was nearly two o'clock when the meeting finished. When he came out, he saw a man running quickly and lightly up the stairs towards him. He was strongly built and broad-shouldered with black hair and a curly beard. Oblonsky smiled with surprise and pleasure.

'Levin! It's you! What are you doing in Moscow?'

Levin and Oblonsky were the same age and had been good

friends since their schooldays. Although they were very fond of one another, they were very different in their characters and tastes. Oblonsky enjoyed the good restaurants and theatres and expensive clothes of Moscow. But town life made Levin feel uncomfortable. He had a large estate and farm in the country, and was only happy when he was living and working there.

'I'm so very glad to see you,' cried Oblonsky, noticing with surprise that Levin was wearing a smart new French suit.

'I must talk to you about something,' said Levin. Suddenly he seemed shy and embarrassed. 'Tell me, what are the Shcherbatskys doing? The same as usual?'

Oblonsky was not at all surprised by Levin's question. He had known for some time that Levin was in love with Princess Kitty Shcherbatskaya, Dolly's younger sister. He smiled.

'If you want to see the Shcherbatskys,' he said, 'they are sure to be in the Skating Gardens from four to five. Kitty skates there. You go, and I'll call for you and we'll have dinner together.'

'Excellent!' said Levin.

At four o'clock that afternoon, Levin went to the Skating Gardens and, with a beating heart, turned along the path to the ice-hills and the skating-ground. He was sure that Kitty would be there as he had seen the Shcherbatskys' carriage at the entrance. It was a bright frosty afternoon, and the ice was crowded with people, young and old, experts and beginners.

Levin recognized Kitty at once among the skaters. He knew she was there by the joy and terror that seized his heart.

Kitty saw him too. She skated up to him, smiling her wonderful smile as she gave him her hand.

'Have you been in Moscow long?' she asked.

'Not long. I came yesterday... I mean today,' said Levin in confusion. 'I didn't know you could skate so well.'

'Why don't you get some skates and we can skate together?' suggested Kitty.

Levin went at once to hire some skates and then joined Kitty on the ice. She took his hand and they set off side by side, going faster and faster, and the faster they skated, the more tightly she grasped his hand. Levin could not speak for happiness.

'Are you in Moscow for long?' Kitty asked.

'I don't know,' replied Levin. Then he added, without thinking, 'It all depends on you.'

At once he noticed a change come over Kitty's face, like the sun disappearing behind a cloud. She either did not hear his words, or did not want to hear. A few minutes later, she skated away from him.

'What have I done?' thought Levin. 'Have I upset her?'

Seeing that Kitty had taken off her skates and was preparing to leave with her mother, Princess Shcherbatskaya, he took off his skates too and went up to them.

'How nice to see you,' said Princess Shcherbatskaya in a polite but cold voice. 'Do come and see us while you are in Moscow. We shall be at home to visitors this evening.'

Later, Levin went with Oblonsky to one of Moscow's most fashionable and expensive restaurants, where all the waiters knew Oblonsky and treated him with the greatest respect. They took his hat and coat, and led him to a special table in a private room.

Levin felt most uncomfortable in this grand restaurant. He preferred the kind of plain simple food that he was used to in the country. But Oblonsky ordered a huge meal for both of them with the most expensive dishes and the finest wines.

'Are you going to the Shcherbatskys tonight?' he asked at the end of the meal.

'Yes. But I'm afraid that Kitty's mother doesn't like me.'

'That's just her manner,' said Oblonsky. 'It doesn't mean anything. But why have you stayed away from Moscow so long? And why have you come back?'

'Why have I come back?' asked Levin, looking at Oblonsky with shining eyes. 'Can't you guess?'

'You're in love with Kitty,' said Oblonsky, smiling.

'Yes,' said Levin. 'I left Moscow because I was afraid I had no chance with her. But I couldn't stop thinking about her. So I've come back to ask if she'll marry me. Do you think there's any possibility she'll say "yes"?'

'Of course,' replied Oblonsky quickly. 'And Dolly believes it too. She's quite sure that Kitty loves you.'

'Really?' cried Levin. 'How wonderful!'

'There's just one thing I ought to tell you,' went on Oblonsky. 'Do you know Count* Vronsky?'

'No, I don't,' replied Levin. 'Why ought I to know him?'

'Because he's one of your rivals. He appeared in Moscow just after you left. He's a young cavalry officer from Petersburg – very rich, handsome and intelligent with a lot of influential connections. Kitty's mother is very keen on him, but I'm sure that Kitty will prefer you to Vronsky. Don't delay any longer. Go quickly and ask her to marry you – and good luck!'

◆

A lot of people were expected at the Shcherbatskys' house that evening. Levin got there early, before any of the other guests had arrived, hoping for the chance to speak to Kitty alone.

Kitty's parents had very different opinions about Levin. Prince Shcherbatsky thought he would make a fine husband for his daughter. But Princess Shcherbatskaya did not think Levin was good enough for Kitty. She disliked his strange opinions and his awkward ways in society, and she had been pleased when he had suddenly left Moscow and gone back to the country.

*Count/Countess: title of a Russian noble

When Vronsky had appeared on the scene, she had been delighted. Vronsky satisfied all her desires for Kitty. He was rich, intelligent and charming and had a brilliant career before him in the army and at Court. He paid Kitty a lot of attention, danced with her at balls, and was always coming to the house. So the Princess was sure that Vronsky's intentions towards Kitty were serious. But he had still not proposed marriage, and as time went by this worried her more and more.

At half past seven that evening, the Shcherbatskys' servant announced Levin. The blood rushed to Kitty's heart and she felt sad and afraid. She knew why Levin had come early, and she knew too that she was going to hurt his feelings. Kitty was very fond of Levin, whom she had known since she was a child, but she thought of him as a brother, not a husband. They were not the same feelings as she had for Vronsky. With him she could imagine a wonderful future of great happiness, but with Levin the future seemed misty and uncertain.

Levin entered the room, looking at her with shining eyes.

'I was hoping to find you alone,' he said. 'I came to say... be my wife!' he finished, not knowing what he was saying.

Kitty was breathing heavily, not looking at him. Her heart was bursting with happiness. She had never expected to feel such a powerful emotion at his words of love. But then she remembered Vronsky, and she looked at Levin's desperate face with her clear, honest eyes.

'No, that cannot be... forgive me,' she replied softly.

For a moment, Levin did not answer. Then he said sadly, 'I understand. No, of course it cannot be.'

He turned to leave, but at that moment Princess Shcherbatskaya came into the room. When she saw Levin's troubled face, she immediately guessed what had happened and felt a great sense of relief.

'Thank God, Kitty has refused him,' she thought.

The other guests began to arrive, and among them was a very handsome and charming dark-haired man in uniform.

'Let me introduce you,' said the Princess to Levin. 'Constantine Dmitrich Levin, Count Alexei Vronsky.'

Vronsky shook Levin's hand and smiled at him warmly.

'I was hoping to meet you earlier,' he said in a friendly way, 'but you had already left Moscow for the country.'

Levin was watching Kitty closely. He saw the way her whole face lit up when she looked at Vronsky, and realized that she loved Vronsky and his own situation was hopeless. He left as soon as he politely could, and his last impression was of Kitty's happy, smiling face as she chatted to Vronsky.

◆

After leaving the Shcherbatskys' house, Levin decided to visit his brother Nikolai.

Nikolai was living in a small hotel. Many years ago he had lived a very religious life, but now he lived in quite a different kind of way. He was drunk for most of the time, and was always getting into trouble with the authorities for his strange and wild behaviour. But in spite of everything, Levin loved Nikolai dearly and wanted to help him.

He had not seen his brother for about three years and he was very shocked by Nikolai's terrible appearance. His brother was suffering from consumption; he was very thin and kept coughing painfully. His face was very pale, with large eyes that were wild and frightened. He greeted Levin with a joy that lit up his face before the suffering returned, and then he introduced a woman standing in the doorway.

'This is my life's companion, Maria. She was working as a prostitute when I met her, and now she looks after me. I love and respect her, and anyone who wishes to know me must love and respect her too. She is the same as a wife to me.'

Maria brought supper for Nikolai and Levin, and Nikolai began to ask questions about their old family home in the country, where Levin still lived. But whenever Levin looked at his brother's thin, pale face, he felt more and more sorry for him.

As he was leaving, he said to Maria, 'Please write to me if you need me. Try to persuade him to come and stay with me.'

The next day, Levin left Moscow and went back to his country estate.

Chapter 2   A Fatal Attraction

At eleven o'clock on the morning after the Shcherbatskys' party, Vronsky drove to the railway station to meet his mother, who was coming to visit him from Petersburg. The first person he saw on the station steps was Oblonsky.

'Who are you meeting?' asked Vronsky, smiling as everyone who met Oblonsky did.

'I've come to meet a pretty woman,' replied Oblonsky. 'My sister Anna.'

'Oh, Karenin's wife?' said Vronsky.

'Yes. You know her, don't you?'

'I think so. Or perhaps not . . . I really don't remember,' replied Vronsky, the name Karenin giving him an indistinct impression of someone rather official and boring.

'But you must know my respected brother-in-law. All the world knows him!'

'Yes, I know him by reputation and by sight. I know that he's clever, and rather religious. But he's not really my type.'

The train had just been signalled. There was a rush of preparation in the station as a crowd of people pushed forward to meet it. The whistle of an engine and the deep, low noise of the train could be heard in the distance. Soon the platform began to shake as the train swung in and at last came to a stop. A young guard jumped out, blowing his whistle, and walked up to Vronsky, who asked him if he knew which carriage the Countess Vronsky was in.

'Yes, she's in that carriage,' replied the guard. Vronsky followed the guard to his mother's carriage, but when he reached the door he had to stop and make way for a lady getting out. He knew at a glance that she belonged to the best society. He felt he must have another look at her – not because of her beauty, but because of something tender in her lovely face. As he looked round, she too turned her head, and her brilliant grey eyes gave him a friendly, curious look.

Vronsky stepped into the carriage. His mother, a dried-up old lady with black eyes and curls, smiled at him with thin lips.

'You got my telegram? You are quite well?'

'Did you have a good journey?' asked Vronsky, sitting down beside her and listening to the sound of a woman's voice outside the door. He knew it was the lady he had just met. She was asking someone about her brother. Then she came back into the carriage.

'Well, have you found your brother?' Vronsky's mother said.

Vronsky realized now that this was Madame Karenina.

'Your brother is here,' he said. He stepped out of the carriage and called for Oblonsky. As soon as Anna saw him, she jumped down from the carriage and ran to him, throwing her arms round his neck and kissing him warmly.

'She is very charming, isn't she?' said the Countess. 'Her husband put her in this carriage with me and we talked for the whole way. She has a little son of eight, and this is the first time they have been separated, and so she is worried about him.'

Anna came back into the carriage to say goodbye.

'Let me kiss your pretty little face, my dear,' said the Countess. 'I can speak plainly at my age, so let me confess that I have lost my heart to you.'

Anna looked delighted. She kissed the Countess, then, with a smile playing round her lips and eyes, offered her little hand to Vronsky. He pressed it, and felt a great joy as she shook it. His eyes followed her as she walked quickly away.

Just as Vronsky and his mother were getting out of the carriage, several men, including the station-master, ran past with frightened faces. It was clear that something unusual had happened. All the passengers were running back to the train.

'What? What? Where? Threw himself under? Run over!' people passing by the window were heard crying. Oblonsky, with his sister on his arm, turned back. They too looked scared, and stopped by the carriage door to avoid the number of people. Anna and Vronsky's mother got back into the carriage, while Vronsky and Oblonsky followed the crowd.

A guard, either too drunk or too wrapped up against the bitter frost to hear anything, had not seen or heard the train as it moved slowly back, and had been crushed to death.

Oblonsky and Vronsky came back to the carriage. They had both seen the guard's mangled body and Oblonsky was looking very upset, as if he was ready to cry.

'Oh, how horrible!' he kept saying. 'Oh, Anna, if you had seen it! And his wife was there too,' he went on. 'It was terrible to see her. She threw herself on his body. They say he has a large family to support. What an awful thing!'

'Is there nothing one could do for her?' whispered Anna.

Vronsky glanced at her and immediately left the carriage. When he returned a few minutes later, Oblonsky was already chatting to the Countess about a new play that had recently been showing in Moscow. They went out together, Vronsky walking ahead with his mother, Anna and her brother following behind. At the exit to the station, the station-master came up to them.

'You gave my assistant a large amount of money,' he said to Vronsky. 'Would you be kind enough to say whom you intended it for?'

'For the widow, of course,' replied Vronsky.

'You gave money?' cried Oblonsky from behind, and pressing his sister's arm, he added, 'Very kind! Very kind!'

When Anna and Oblonsky came out of the station, the Vronskys had already driven off. As Anna sat down in the carriage, Oblonsky noticed with surprise that her lips were trembling and she had difficulty in keeping back her tears.

'What's the matter, Anna?' he asked.

'That guard's death is a bad omen,' she said.

'Nonsense!' replied Oblonsky. 'You've come, that's the main thing. You cannot imagine how I'm depending on you to make things better between Dolly and me.'

'Have you known Vronsky long?' asked Anna.

'Yes. You know, we're hoping he'll marry Kitty.'

'Really?' said Anna softly. 'Now let's talk about your affairs,' she added, as if she wanted to shake off something that was troubling her. 'Tell me all about your problems.'

And Oblonsky began his story. When they got home, he helped his sister out of the carriage, pressed her hand and drove off to the courthouse.

Although Dolly had told her husband that she did not care if Anna came or not, she had made everything ready for Anna's arrival and was waiting for her anxiously.

'After all, it's not Anna's fault,' thought Dolly. 'I know only good of her, and she has only ever shown me kindness and friendship.'

All these days Dolly had been alone with the children. She did not want to talk about her troubles, but she also knew that she would tell Anna everything. When she heard the sound of Anna's light footsteps outside the door, she went to kiss her.

'Dolly, I'm so glad to see you!' cried Anna.

Anna admired all Dolly's children, then started to talk to Dolly about Oblonsky. She listened to Dolly with sympathetic kindness, and soon Dolly began to feel much better.

'What shall I do? Please, Anna, help me.'

'Listen, Dolly, Stiva is still in love with you. I'm his sister and I know his character. He wasn't in love with this other woman – he didn't betray you in his heart.'

'But it might happen again! Would *you* forgive it?'

'I don't think it will happen again. But, yes,' said Anna, after thinking for a moment. 'Yes, I would forgive it.'

Finally, Anna persuaded Dolly to forgive Oblonsky. That evening, Oblonsky had dinner at home and Dolly spoke to him, calling him 'Stiva' – which she had not done since the quarrel.

Immediately after dinner, Kitty arrived. She knew Anna, but only slightly, and was a little worried about what this fashionable lady from Petersburg would think of her. But it was soon obvious that Anna admired Kitty's youth and beauty very much. Kitty was very attracted by Anna. Anna did not look like a society lady, or the mother of an eight-year-old son, but more like a girl of twenty.

'There's going to be a grand ball next week,' said Kitty excitedly. 'Are you going to come?'

'I suppose I shall have to,' replied Anna, smiling. 'But balls are no fun for me any more.' Then she continued, 'I know something – Stiva told me and I congratulate you. I met Vronsky at the railway station and I liked him very much.'

'Oh, was he there?' asked Kitty, laughing and turning red. 'What did Stiva tell you?'

◆

The ball was just beginning when Kitty and her mother climbed the wide stairs, brilliantly lit and covered with flowers, that led up to the ballroom. They could hear the sound of the violins starting the first dance. Kitty was looking lovely as she entered the room in her beautiful pink dress. Everything about her was perfect – her shoes, her beautiful thick hair and a charming black velvet ribbon round her neck – and she attracted many glances of admiration.

At once the leading dancer there, Korsunsky, the famous and handsome 'master-of-ceremonies', came up to her and put his arm round her waist. She bent her left arm and placed her hand on his shoulder. Her little feet in their pink dancing-shoes moved lightly over the polished floor, in time with the music.

'It's delightful to dance with you,' said her partner. 'Where shall I take you?' he added, as the music finished.

Kitty had seen that the most important people in society were grouped together in a corner of the room. Among them she saw Stiva, and Anna's lovely head and beautiful figure, dressed in black velvet. And *he* was there. Vronsky. Kitty had not seen him since the evening she had refused Levin.

'There's Madame Karenina – will you take me to her?'

As Kitty approached the little group, Anna turned to her with a tender, protective smile, nodding her approval of Kitty's dress and pretty appearance.

Vronsky came up to Kitty and asked her to dance. They did not talk about anything of importance, but Kitty was not worried. She was waiting with beating heart for the most important dance of the evening – the mazurka. She was sure that she would dance the mazurka with Vronsky and that, while they were dancing, he would propose marriage.

After the dance had finished, Kitty had to dance with several boring young men whom she could not refuse. During one of these dances, she came face to face with Anna dancing with Vronsky.

Anna was looking very happy and excited. Every time Vronsky spoke to her, her eyes lit up with joy and there was a smile of happiness on her red lips. Kitty looked at Vronsky, and was suddenly filled with fear. The expression on Anna's face was mirrored in Vronsky's.

A mist spread over Kitty's soul, shutting out the ball and all the world. She had to go on dancing, smiling and politely answering her partner's questions. But while the ballroom was being prepared for the mazurka, she suffered terror and despair. She knew that Vronsky would not ask her for the mazurka. He was going to dance it with Anna.

From across the room, Kitty saw Vronsky and Anna sitting almost opposite her. Later, when dancing the mazurka with Korsunsky, she met them in the dance. The more she looked, the more she realized that something had happened between them, and that everything was finished for her. Anna looked so charming in her simple black dress, with her curls and lovely animated face. Kitty admired her more than ever, and suffered more and more. She felt crushed, and her face showed it. When she came up against Vronsky in the dance, her expression had changed so much that at first he did not recognize her.

'A delightful ball!' he said, as if talking to a stranger.

Later in the dance, Anna and Kitty found themselves dancing side by side. Anna smiled and pressed Kitty's hand, but seeing that Kitty only responded to her smile with a look of surprise and despair, she turned away.

After the dance, Anna did not want to stay to supper.

'I have danced more in Moscow at this one ball of yours than I have the whole winter in Petersburg. I must go home and rest before my journey,' she told Vronsky.

'So you really are going tomorrow?' he asked.

'Yes, I think so,' Anna replied. Her eyes shone and her smile set him on fire as she spoke the words.

Chapter 3   Passion

Early on the morning after the ball, Anna sent her husband a telegram to say that she was leaving Moscow that same day.

'I must go,' she told Dolly, explaining the change in her plans. 'And I'll confess the reason to you now. I've spoiled everything

15

for Kitty with Vronsky. She's jealous of me and I made the ball a torture for her. But, really, it's not my fault – or only a little bit.'

'You sound exactly like Stiva!' said Dolly. 'Remember, Anna, I'll never forget what you've done for me and Stiva. I'll always love you as my dearest friend!'

That night, when Anna was on the train to Petersburg, she felt great pleasure and relief to be going home.

'Tomorrow I'll see Seriozha and my husband, and my nice everyday life will go on as before,' she thought.

There was a terrible storm outside, and snow beat against the window of the train. Anna was trying to read a novel, but she could not concentrate on it so she listened to the noise of the train as it rushed on through the dark night. After some time, she realized they had stopped at a station.

It was very hot in the carriage. Anna opened the door and felt a cold rush of wind and snow. The wind seemed to be trying to carry her off, but with a strong hand she felt for the cold handrail and stepped down on to the platform. She filled her lungs with deep breaths of snowy, frosty air, looking round at the platform and the lighted station.

A man wearing a military overcoat stepped close to her, and Anna at once recognized Vronsky. As he bowed to her and asked if he could be of service, she saw that his face had the same expression of great joy as at the ball.

'I didn't know you were travelling. What are you coming to Petersburg for?' she asked, her face shining with joy.

'What am I coming for?' he repeated, looking straight into her eyes. 'You know that I have come to be where you are.'

At that moment the wind sent the snow flying from the carriage roof. The awful storm now seemed more beautiful than terrible to Anna. Vronsky's words had made her feel both happy and afraid, and for a long time she made no reply.

'You should not say that and I beg of you, if you are a gentleman, to forget it, as I will forget it,' she said at last. She took

16

hold of the handrail, and climbed up the steps into the train, where she did not sleep all night, thinking of Vronsky.

The next morning, when the train arrived in Petersburg, the first person whom Anna saw on the platform was the cold, proud figure of her husband. Catching sight of her, he came forward, his large tired eyes looking straight at her. A disagreeable sensation pressed down on her heart.

'You see, here is your loving husband, burning with impatience to see you,' he said in his slow, thin voice.

'Is Seriozha all right?' asked Anna.

'Yes, he is quite all right, quite all right . . .'

Vronsky, too, had noticed Karenin. For the first time he clearly realized that there was someone, a husband, attached to Anna. He only fully believed in Karenin's existence when he saw his head and shoulders, and his legs in their black trousers; and especially when Karenin calmly took Anna's hand with an air of ownership. He, too, experienced a disagreeable sensation.

'She does not love him, she cannot love him,' he decided.

'Did you have a good night?' he asked, going up to Anna.

'Excellent, thank you,' she replied. Her face looked tired, but as she glanced at him her eyes lit up. She turned to her husband to find out if he knew Vronsky. Karenin looked at him with displeasure, trying to remember who this was.

'Count Vronsky,' said Anna.

'Ah, we have met before,' said Karenin without emotion.

'I hope I may call on you?' Vronsky asked Anna.

Karenin looked at Vronsky in a tired way.

'Delighted,' he said coldly. 'We are at home on Mondays.' Then, dismissing Vronsky, he started talking to Anna.

Anna's son, Seriozha, was very pleased to see his mother again. She told him all about Dolly's children and gave him presents. Later, friends visited her and gave her the news of everything that had happened in Petersburg during her absence. Anna spent the rest of the day unpacking and answering letters.

'Nothing happened,' she told herself. 'Vronsky said something silly to me, and I answered as I should have done. I must not tell my husband about it, and there is no need to.'

That evening Karenin had to go out to a meeting, so after she had put Seriozha to bed, Anna sat down quietly by the fire with her novel and waited for him. At half past nine he returned. He had tea with Anna and talked a little to her about things in Moscow, then went to his study to work. Later, as Anna was sitting at her desk finishing a letter to Dolly, he came into her room.

'Time for bed now,' he said with a special smile, crossing into the bedroom. Anna got up and followed him, but there was no animation in her eyes or smile.

◆

Anna had many friends among the most influential people in Petersburg society. She went to many balls, operas and dinner parties, and whenever he could, Vronsky went to places where he knew Anna would be. Every time they met, joy lit up her eyes and her heart beat with the same feeling of animation that had seized her on the train the first day she saw him. Soon she realized that Vronsky was the whole interest of her life.

One evening, Anna met Vronsky at the house of her cousin's wife, the Princess Betsy Tverskaya.

'I must talk to you privately,' she said to him. At once he sat down on a sofa beside her. 'I've just had a letter from Moscow. Kitty Shcherbatskaya is really ill. You behaved badly, very badly indeed. You knew very well she was expecting you to propose marriage. Go to Moscow and beg her forgiveness.'

'You don't wish that,' he said softly. 'Don't you know that you are my life, my whole being, my love. To me, you and I are one. And I do not see any possibility of peace ahead for us – only of despair, unhappiness . . . or happiness, what happiness! Can it be there's no chance of it?' he whispered.

Anna's friendship with Vronsky became the subject of much gossip among Princess Betsy's friends and the rest of Petersburg's fashionable society. Karenin, too, had noticed his wife's behaviour. Although he worried about what people might think, he decided that his best course of action would be to ignore it.

So Vronsky and Anna became lovers. Vronsky's whole inner life was centred round his feelings for Anna, but there was little change in his daily routine. His army regiment was still very important to him; he was fond of it, and the soldiers in the regiment respected him and were proud of him.

He never spoke of his love for Anna to the other officers, not even when he had been drinking. But in spite of that, his love was known to all the town. Many of the younger officers admired Vronsky and were jealous of him, mainly because Karenin had such an important position in society.

Vronsky's mother was pleased at first when she heard about his relationship with Anna, because she thought that an affair in high society would bring new opportunities to her brilliant young son. But when she learned that he had refused a post of great importance to his career because he wanted to stay in Petersburg to be near Anna, and that important people were angry with him, she changed her mind.

Apart from his regiment and society, Vronsky had another great passion – horses. There was going to be an officers' race and he had bought a fine English horse to ride.

On the day of the race Vronsky decided to go and see Anna. He knew she was staying at the Karenins' summer house a few kilometres outside Petersburg, and that Karenin had just returned from abroad but was staying in their town house. He drove in a carriage out to the summer house.

Anna was sitting in a corner of the terrace behind some flowers. The beauty of her figure, her dark, curly hair, her neck, her arms, struck him with a new surprise and he stood still, staring at her in great joy. She felt his presence and, as she turned to face him, he saw that her face looked hot and red.

'What's the matter? Are you ill?' he said, going up to her.

'No, I'm all right,' she replied, pressing his hand tightly. 'I didn't expect you. I'm alone and I was waiting for Seriozha. He's gone out for a walk.'

'But you're ill or worried,' he went on, not letting her hand go but bending over her. 'What were you thinking about? Tell me. I can see that something has happened.'

'I'm pregnant,' Anna whispered slowly. Vronsky's hands shook, but she did not remove her eyes from his face. He turned pale, tried to say something, but stopped and dropped her hand, then started walking up and down the terrace.

'We must put an end to the deceit in which we are living,' he said at last. 'You must tell your husband everything and leave him, so that our lives can be united.'

'But, Alexei, do you know what the result will be?' Anna asked. 'He will say that he cannot let me disgrace his name; he will say in his official manner that he cannot let me go but will do everything possible to prevent a scandal. He's not a human being but a machine, and a cruel machine when he's angry.'

'We have to tell him,' said Vronsky, trying to calm her.

'And what shall we do afterwards? Shall we run away?'

'Yes, why not? We can't go on like this.'

Vronsky could not understand why Anna did not want to escape from their state of deceit. He did not guess that her main reason was her son. What would happen to Seriozha? And she could not bear the thought of his opinion of her if she lived as the mistress of a man who was not his father.

'I know all the horror of my position,' said Anna, 'but things are not so easy to arrange as you think.'

◆

Seventeen officers, their faces pale and serious, were taking part in the race. Vronsky sat on his horse, Frou-Frou, at the starting point, looking round at his rivals. He knew that Anna and her husband were among the crowd of fashionable people who were preparing to watch the race.

The starter shouted 'Off!' and the race began.

Frou-Frou was going very well. Some of the horses fell at the first jump, but Frou-Frou flew over it as if she had wings.

'Oh, you beauty!' thought Vronsky. He felt the eyes of the crowd on him from all sides, but he saw nothing except the ears and neck of his horse. Now Vronsky had the lead and he felt confident of success. His excitement and happiness grew as Frou-Frou flew over each jump perfectly. He heard the voices of soldiers in his regiment shouting his name.

Now there was only one jump left – the water jump. Frou-Frou cleared it easily, like a bird, but at that moment Vronsky made a terrible mistake. Instead of moving his body forward with the horse, he sat back in the saddle. At once his position changed and he knew that something horrible had happened. His unexpected movement had made Frou-Frou lose her balance and she was falling. Another horse flashed by him. Vronsky was touching the ground with one foot as the horse fell on top of him. His clumsy movement had broken her back. He managed to free himself but Frou-Frou sank to the ground.

'What have I done?' Vronsky cried. 'The race is lost, and it was all my own fault. And my poor, dear horse!'

People ran up to him from all sides, including a doctor and officers of his regiment. Vronsky was unhurt, but the horse had to be shot. Vronsky could not speak to anyone. He walked off the racecourse, not knowing where he was going. The memory of that race remained in his heart for a long time, the cruellest and most bitter memory of his life.

Karenin had been sitting near Anna when the race began. He looked at her and saw that her face was pale and very anxious. Clearly she was seeing nothing and nobody except one man, and at that moment Karenin read on her face with horror the love which he did not wish to know about. When Vronsky fell, Anna cried out aloud.

'Let us go, let us go!' she screamed, jumping to her feet.

Karenin approached her and offered her his arm, but Anna moved away from him with a look of hate. She was staring at the place where Vronsky had fallen, but there was such a crowd of people that she could not see anything clearly. She was ready to go to Vronsky, when an officer ran towards them. He brought news that Vronsky was not dead but that the horse had broken her back. When she heard this, Anna sat down and hid her face and cried with relief.

'I'm offering you my arm,' Karenin said coldly. 'Let us go.' Anna left the racecourse as if in a dream, all the time thinking of Vronsky. She took her seat in her husband's carriage in silence.

As they drove away, Karenin said, 'Your behaviour today was highly inappropriate.'

'In what way?'

'The despair you could not hide when one of the riders fell.' He waited for her to answer, but she was silent. She was only half listening to him; she could not think of anything except Vronsky and if it was true that he was not dead. 'Possibly I have made a mistake,' Karenin added.

'No,' said Anna slowly, looking with despair into his cold face. 'You have not made a mistake. I am listening to you, but I am thinking of him. I love him and I am his mistress. I hate you, I am afraid of you ... You can do what you like with me.'

Chapter 4   Life in the Country

After her rejection by Vronsky at the ball, Kitty had become very ill and depressed. On the advice of doctors, her worried parents took her abroad to Europe for a few months, hoping the change of scene would help her. Slowly her health improved, and she eventually returned home to Russia cured. She was not so carefree or light-hearted as before, but she was at peace.

Meanwhile, Levin was working hard on his country estate. It was still very painful to him to think about Kitty's refusal. After dreaming for so long of family life and feeling so ready for it, he was still single and farther than ever from marriage. He was very conscious, as were all around him, that it was not good for a man of his age to be alone. But the place in his heart was taken by Kitty, and it was impossible for him to imagine there any of the other girls he knew.

But the passing of time, and the ordinary but important events of country life helped him. To Levin, the country was the solid base for life – the place where one was happy, suffered and did good and useful work. He was particularly concerned with how he could get the best out of the peasants who worked for him on his farm. He recognized that, to make the farm most profitable, he needed the peasants to work with him, not against him.

He was a good-hearted man, but he did not have idealistic views about the peasants – he was angry when they were careless, or got drunk or lied to him. Levin worked hard, and he expected the peasants to work hard too; during the long summer days he sometimes helped them in the fields.

A few weeks after a short visit from Oblonsky, during which Levin learnt that Kitty was not married to Vronsky but had been very ill, he received a letter from his friend. Oblonsky wrote that Dolly and the children were staying for the summer at the Shcherbatskys' country house, which was about forty kilometres from Levin's estate. Oblonsky himself could not join them because he had to stay in town for business. He asked Levin if he could ride over and see Dolly, who was alone, and give her any help and advice she needed.

Levin replied that he would be delighted to visit Dolly, whom he had always thought of as a very nice person.

The Shcherbatskys' country house needed a lot of repairs. Dolly had begged Oblonsky to look over the house before they arrived, and to get the repairs done. Oblonsky had given instructions for things which he thought necessary, such as re-covering the furniture, putting up curtains, planting flowers and building a little bridge by the lake. But he had forgotten many other things which were essential, and which were now causing great problems for Dolly.

On his return to Moscow, Oblonsky had told Dolly proudly that he had taken care of everything. The departure of his wife to the country suited him very well. It would be good for the children, it would save money and it would leave him free. Dolly also regarded a move to the country as of great benefit to the children. She hoped, too, that her sister Kitty would join them there.

But Dolly found the first few days of life in the country very difficult. It rained a lot, things in the house did not work, she could not get local servants to help her, and there was something wrong with the cows and chickens so that she and her children did not have enough butter or eggs. Dolly was in despair. Her childhood memories of the country were of a happy, relaxed place with no troubles or cares, but this was quite the opposite!

Fortunately, Dolly had brought her old nurse from Moscow, who was a very efficient and useful person. She calmed Dolly, worked hard, and within a week had got the local people to help and most of the problems solved. But by this time, Dolly's desperate letters had reached her husband. Although Oblonsky promised to come down at the first opportunity, after a month the opportunity had still not presented itself, so meanwhile he wrote to Levin, asking him to go and help her.

Things were once again going badly in Dolly and Oblonsky's marriage. The peace following their quarrel over the French teacher had not lasted, and Oblonsky had soon returned to his old ways, following a life of pleasure and chasing new mistresses. Dolly knew that her husband did not love her, but her chief source of pleasure was her five children.

One afternoon, Dolly decided to take the children to the river to bathe. They had such a wonderful time that Dolly, who was fond of bathing too, had never felt happier.

As they got back home, a servant came out and told them that a gentleman was coming. Dolly was delighted to see Levin's familiar figure approaching. When he looked at her, he found himself face to face with a picture of the family life of his dreams.

'I'm so glad to see you,' said Dolly.

'I had a note from Stiva telling me you were here.'

'From Stiva?' said Dolly in surprise.

'Yes. He thought perhaps I could help you,' replied Levin, suddenly embarrassed as he thought that Dolly might not like to accept help which should have come from her own husband.

'Oh, thank you, things were difficult at first, but we're fine now, thanks to my old nurse,' replied Dolly, smiling brightly.

Levin spent a very happy and relaxed day at the house. He played with the children, who all loved him. After dinner, when they were sitting alone on the balcony, Dolly said, 'You know, Kitty is coming here to spend the summer.'

'Really?' said Levin, his face changing colour. He longed passionately, but was also afraid, to hear more about Kitty.

'And how is she – better?' he asked nervously.

'Yes, thank God, she's quite well. Let me ask you something – are you angry with her?'

'No,' said Levin, turning red to the roots of his hair. 'I'm not angry with her. But you know that I made her an offer of marriage and was refused.'

'Really?' said Dolly. 'I guessed, but I wasn't sure. Now I understand why she was so unhappy. I see it all.'

'Well,' said Levin, getting up, 'I have to go now.'

'No, wait,' said Dolly. 'Sit down and listen. At the time that you made an offer to Kitty, she did not know her state of mind. She was hesitating – hesitating between you and Vronsky. She was seeing him every day, she had not seen you for some time. If only she had been older . . . I never liked Vronsky.'

Levin thought about the answer which Kitty had given him. She had said, '*No, that cannot be . . .*'

'I will say only one thing more,' Dolly went on. 'I don't say Kitty cares for you; but her refusal at that moment doesn't mean anything.'

'I don't know!' cried Levin, jumping to his feet again. 'If you only knew how you are hurting me! It's as if you had a child who died, and people keep saying, "He would have been like this, and like that, and how happy you would have been with him." But he's dead, dead, dead!'

'How ridiculous you are!' said Dolly, smiling. 'Yes, I see it all clearly. So you won't come to see us when Kitty is here?'

'No,' said Levin. 'No, I shan't come.'

◆

Levin had often admired the simple life of the peasants and envied the men who lived it. He had sometimes thought about exchanging the selfish, complicated life he was leading, with all its problems and responsibilities, for a simple, honest life of hard work. Now, for the first time, having lost all hope of Kitty, he began to think about marrying a peasant girl.

One day, he worked hard in the fields, had supper with the

peasants and then spent the night in the open air. In the early morning he got up, looked at the fading stars and saw that the night was over.

'What am I going to do?' he thought. 'Give up my old life? Marry a peasant girl? How can I begin? All my old dreams of family life were nonsense . . . I must start again.'

Levin began to walk quickly along the road towards the nearest village, his eyes fixed on the ground. Suddenly, he heard the sound of carriage bells.

'Someone's coming,' he thought. He glanced at the carriage as it went by and saw a young girl inside, clearly just awake, looking towards the sunrise. It was she. It was Kitty on her way to the Shcherbatskys' country house.

Immediately Levin forgot everything he had thought about during the night. The idea of marrying a peasant girl disgusted him. The barking of the dogs told him that the carriage had reached the village. All that was left were the empty fields and himself, making his way along the lonely road.

He looked up at the sky. Everything was blue and clear.

'No,' he said to himself, 'however good a life of simple hard work may be, I cannot go back to it. I love *her*.'

Chapter 5   Karenin's Decision

When Anna told her husband that she was in love with Vronsky, her words struck a cruel blow to Karenin's heart. He took her back to the summer house, helped her out of the carriage and, making an effort to control himself, said goodbye with his usual calm and told her that he would inform her of his decision the next day.

'She has no honour, no heart, no religion,' he thought. 'I made a mistake when I linked my life to hers; but I cannot be blamed for my mistake, and therefore I will not be unhappy; I am not the guilty one – *she* is.'

Whatever might happen to Anna and her son, towards whom his feelings were as much changed as towards her, ceased to interest Karenin.

'I have to find the best way out of the painful situation in which she has placed me,' he thought to himself, his face growing darker and darker. He considered how other men who had found themselves in a similar situation had dealt with it.

'I could fight a duel . . .'

In his youth, the idea of a duel had very much interested Karenin for the reason that he was physically a coward and quite aware of it. He could not think without horror of a gun being pointed at him, and had never handled one in his life.

'Suppose I learn to shoot,' he said to himself, 'and I kill Vronsky. What sense is there in murdering him? I would still have to decide what to do with my wife. But what is more likely to happen is that *I*, the innocent person, would be the victim.'

Having rejected the idea of a duel, Karenin's thoughts turned to divorce. He thought about all the cases he knew of divorce, but he could not find a single example in which the purpose of the divorce was the one he had in mind. He had a high position in society and a divorce would only lead to scandal. Moreover, in spite of the complete lack of interest that he now imagined he had in his wife, he did not want to set her free so she could be with Vronsky and profit from her crime.

'Apart from formal divorce, we could just separate,' he thought. But this step presented the same problem of public scandal as a divorce, and it, too, would throw his wife into the arms of Vronsky. 'No, it's impossible,' he said aloud. 'I must not be unhappy, but neither she nor he must be happy!'

Jealous at first, Karenin's desire now was that Anna should be punished for her crime. In the depths of his soul, but without admitting it to himself, he wanted her to suffer for having destroyed his peace of mind and his honour. And having rejected the idea of a duel, a divorce and a separation, Karenin decided there was only one solution. He would keep Anna with him, hiding what had happened from the world and using all his power to break off the affair and to punish her.

Karenin felt pleased with his decision. He then thought of another important reason in support of it.

'This is the only course of action suited to my religious principles,' he told himself. 'I'm not getting rid of a guilty wife, but giving her a chance to mend her ways.'

Karenin drove back to Petersburg. When he arrived home, he immediately went into his study and wrote a letter to Anna.

> *During our last conversation, I informed you of my intention to communicate to you my decision. Whatever your behaviour may have been, I do not consider I have the right to cut the ties with which a Higher Power has joined us. The family cannot be broken up because of the sin of one of the partners, and our life must continue as before. I am sure that you are sorry about your behaviour, and you will not continue with it. If you do, you can imagine what the future holds for you and your son. I ask you to return to Petersburg as soon as possible, not later than Tuesday. All necessary preparations will be made for your arrival. A. Karenin*

Karenin put the letter in an envelope with money for his wife's expenses and rang the bell for a servant.

'Have this delivered by special messenger to my wife at the summer house,' he said, getting up.

Then Karenin ordered tea in his study and started work. There were many important things happening in his official life, and he had a great opportunity to serve the Government and to advance his career. Then he glanced at a portrait of Anna on the wall, a beautiful painting by a famous artist. But after a minute or two he could not bear to look at it any longer, and turned away.

◆

Anna was glad that she had told her husband the truth, in spite of the great pain it had caused her. She told herself that now there would be no more lies or deceit. It seemed to her beyond doubt that her position would be made clear for ever; it might be bad, but it would be clear and not false.

But when she awoke next morning, the first thing that came into her mind was what she had said to her husband, and her words seemed so awful that she did not know how she could have spoken them. Now her position, which the night before had seemed simple, seemed hopeless. What terrible things would her husband do? Would he turn her out of the house, so her disgrace would be clear to all the world?

When she thought of Vronsky, it seemed to her that he did not love her, that he was already beginning to find her a burden, and she felt bitter against him for it.

Her maid came in with Anna's clothes and a note from Princess Betsy, inviting Anna to a party later that day.

'Seriozha is waiting downstairs,' she added.

The thought of her son brought Anna out of the helpless state in which she found herself. No matter what might happen to her, she could not give up her son. She must take him and go away.

She dressed quickly and went downstairs. Seriozha and his teacher were waiting for her to start breakfast. She took hold of Seriozha and kissed him. She felt tears coming into her eyes and, to hide them, she jumped up and went out on to the terrace.

Standing still and looking at the tops of the trees waving in the wind, and their rain-washed leaves shining brightly in the cold sunshine, Anna knew that society would not forgive her. 'I must get ready to leave,' she thought. 'I'll go to Moscow by the evening train and take Seriozha with me.' She went inside to tell the servants.

Then she heard the noise of carriage wheels approaching. She looked out of the window and saw Karenin's messenger on the steps, ringing at the bell. A few minutes later, a servant brought in an envelope addressed in her husband's writing.

Anna opened the envelope with trembling fingers and the letter and the money fell out. When she had finished reading, she felt cold all over. Karenin's letter was more awful than anything she had imagined.

'He's in the right!' she cried. 'Of course, he's always in the right! People say he's so religious, so clever; but they don't know how for eight years he's crushed my life, crushed everything that was living in me – he has never once thought that I'm a live woman in need of love.

' "... *you can imagine what the future holds for you and your son* ..." That's a threat to take Seriozha away from me. He knows that I would not give up my son, that there could be no life for me without my child, even with the man I love. He knows that.

' "*Our life must continue as before...*" That life was miserable enough in the past; what will it be like now? And he knows all that, he knows that I can't be sorry, that only lies and deceit will be the result. But it's a torture for me and I can't live with it; anything is better than lying and deceit. Oh God! Oh God! Was a woman ever as unhappy as I am?'

Anna jumped up and went to the writing table to reply to Karenin. But at the bottom of her heart she knew that she would not have the strength to change anything, or to escape from the old situation, however false and dishonourable it was.

She sat down, laid her head on her hands and cried like a child. She knew that everything would go on as it was – would, in fact, be much worse than before. She would not have the courage to find freedom in love, but would always be the guilty wife, deceiving her husband for the sake of a disgraceful affair with a man whose life she could never share.

The servant came back into the room.

'The messenger is waiting for an answer,' he said.

Anna went to the table and wrote, '*I have received your letter – A*'. Then she gave the letter to the servant and rang for her maid to tell her she was not going to Moscow. She wrote a note to Vronsky, asking him to meet her that afternoon in the Vrede Gardens.

◆

Vronsky had a code of principles which defined with absolute certainty what should and should not be done. This code said, for example, that one must not lie to a man but could lie to a woman; that one must never cheat anyone but one could cheat a husband; that one must never forgive an insult but could insult others oneself. Only lately, in regard to Anna, had Vronsky felt that his code did not cover all circumstances.

His present relationship with Anna and her husband was perfectly clear and simple in his mind. She was an honourable woman who had given him her love; therefore she was in his eyes a woman who had a right to the same respect as a lawful wife. From the moment that Anna gave him her love, Vronsky considered that he and not her husband had rights over her. The only right her husband had was to challenge him to a duel.

Anna's news that she was pregnant had frightened Vronsky. He had felt that his code of principles did not cover this situation, but his heart had told him to beg her to leave her husband.

'But if she leaves her husband, that means joining her life with mine,' he thought. 'And how can I take her away, when I will have no income if I leave the army?'

Nobody except himself knew that Vronsky was a very ambitious man. He had been very successful, until he had mistakenly refused an important post that was offered to him.

Meanwhile an old schoolfriend of his, Serpuhovsky, who was of the same age and background as Vronsky, and had joined the army at the same time, was doing extremely well. Serpuhovsky had just returned from Central Asia, where he had become a great general after two promotions.

Everybody in Petersburg was talking about him. He was expecting a high command which might even have an influence on the course of political events. Vronsky, although independent and brilliant, and loved by a charming woman, was only a captain of cavalry.

The army was holding a big party in Serpuhovsky's honour at a large country house. It was three years since Vronsky had seen Serpuhovsky; he was still handsome, but his success had also given him a certain gentleness and nobility.

Serpuhovsky was delighted to see his old friend. Vronsky congratulated him on his success, and the two friends began to talk. Serpuhovsky had heard about Vronsky's relationship with Anna but he did not mention it openly.

'I heard about your refusal of promotion,' he said. 'You didn't do it in quite the right way.'

'I'm happy as I am,' replied Vronsky. 'I don't have the desire for power.'

'That's not true,' said Serpuhovsky, smiling. 'You do have it. And I can help you get a better position.'

'But I don't want anything,' replied Vronsky.

'Listen, we're the same age. Perhaps you've known more women than I have. Women are the chief reasons for failure in a man's career. It's difficult to love a woman and do anything.'

'You have never loved,' said Vronsky quietly, staring straight before him and thinking of Anna.

'Perhaps not. But remember what I've told you.'

Just then a servant approached Vronsky with the note from Anna, asking him to meet her in the Vrede Gardens. He opened the note and his face went red.

'My head aches. I'm going home,' he said.

'Well, goodbye, then. But let's continue this conversation another time. I'll come and see you in Petersburg.'

Vronsky took a carriage at once to the Vrede Gardens. He was feeling pleased with his conversation with Serpuhovsky, and he was looking forward to seeing Anna. The August day was bright and cold, and the cool air made his neck and face feel fresh. When the carriage arrived at the Gardens, he jumped out and went to look for Anna. He saw her walking, and a thrill ran through his body like an electric current.

'You're not angry that I sent for you? I absolutely had to see you,' she said, pressing his hand. 'I must talk to you.'

'What is it? What's happened?' he asked.

She walked on a few steps in silence, gathering up her courage, then suddenly stopped.

'I told my husband everything,' she said. 'I told him I could no longer be his wife.'

'Yes, that's better, a thousand times better!' he cried, and a proud, serious expression came over his face.

Anna could not guess from his expression that Vronsky was thinking that a duel was now inevitable. The possibility of a duel had never crossed her mind, so she did not understand the reason for his serious look. She had hoped that this meeting with Vronsky would change their position and save her, but now she saw that things would continue in the same old way.

'Read this,' she said, showing him Karenin's letter.

Vronsky, meanwhile, was imagining the challenge that would be waiting at home for him from Karenin.

'I'm very happy!' cried Vronsky, 'Things can't go on as he supposes.'

'Why not?' asked Anna.

Vronsky meant that after the inevitable duel things would have to change, but what he said was, 'I hope that you will leave him.'

'And my son?' cried Anna. 'You see what he writes? I would have to leave my son, and I can't and won't do that.'

'Is divorce really not possible?' asked Vronsky. Anna shook her head. 'Couldn't you take your son, and still leave your husband?'

'Yes, but it all depends on him. Now I must go to him.'

Anna's carriage, which she had sent away and ordered to come back to the Vrede Gardens, drove up. She said goodbye to Vronsky and went back to the summer house.

In his letter, Karenin had asked Anna to return from the summer house to their Petersburg house on Tuesday. But he had been so busy with official business that he had completely forgotten about her, and was annoyed when a servant came to tell him she had arrived with Seriozha.

He did not leave his study, but sent a servant to say that he was busy with his secretary. Anna sent Seriozha to his room, then went to her room and started to unpack, expecting that Karenin would come. But an hour passed, and he did not come.

She heard his secretary leave, and knew that he would soon be going to his office in his usual way. She wanted to see him before he left, so she went to his study, and found him sitting at his desk in his official uniform, looking at some papers. He got up, took her hand and asked her to sit down.

'I am very glad you are here,' he said. 'Is Seriozha well? I shall not be dining at home today, and I have to go out now.'

'I am a guilty woman,' began Anna, 'I am a bad woman, but I am the same as I was, as I told you then, and I have come to say that I cannot alter anything.'

'That is what I assumed,' he said. 'But I shall ignore your behaviour as long as the world knows nothing about it, and my name is not disgraced. Our relationship must remain the same.'

'But it cannot be the same,' said Anna in a thin voice. 'I cannot be your wife while I . . . What is it you want of me?'

Karenin gave a cold, spiteful laugh.

'I want not to meet that man here, and I want you to behave so that neither society nor the servants can find anything to say against you . . . I want you not to see him. I think that is not too much to ask. In return, you will enjoy all the privileges of a respectable wife without having to perform any of the duties.'

He got up and moved towards the door. Anna got up, too. Bowing to her in silence, he let her pass.

Chapter 6   A Visit from Nikolai

Levin knew that Kitty was staying with Dolly, just forty kilometres away from his farm, and he wanted to see her but could not. He knew now that he had never ceased to love Kitty, but he could not go over to Dolly's place, knowing that she was there. He had proposed marriage, and she had refused him, and that had placed a barrier between them.

'I can't ask her to be my wife only because she can't be the wife of the man she wanted to marry,' he said to himself. The thought of this made him feel cold and angry towards her. 'And, besides, how can I now, after what Dolly told me, go to see them? It's impossible, impossible!'

Dolly sent him a note, asking him for the loan of a saddle for Kitty's horse. 'I hope you will bring it over yourself,' she wrote. Levin wrote a dozen answers and tore them all up, eventually sending the saddle without any reply. The next day, he set off to visit an old friend in a distant part of the country.

Levin had lately been feeling very dissatisfied with the way he was managing his life and his farm. During his conversations with his friend, he realized that for his farm to be successful, he had to interest the peasants in its success too, by offering them land and giving them a share of the profits.

He returned home full of enthusiasm and plans. At first, the peasants were not very interested in listening to his ideas;

they were too busy trying to get their work done. But when they did at last understand what Levin was saying, they agreed to take shares in the farm. Levin, hopeful that the new system would work, divided up his land among different families of peasants.

The new arrangements on his farm kept him busy for the whole summer. He read many books about estate management, and planned to journey abroad in the autumn to study land systems further. At the end of August, he heard from a servant who brought back the saddle that Dolly and her children had returned to Moscow with Kitty.

One evening at the end of September, Levin was working in his study when he heard the sound of a carriage outside. As he ran downstairs, he heard the sound of coughing. The tall, thin man taking off his fur coat was his brother, Nikolai.

Nikolai stood in the hall, pulling a scarf from his long, thin neck and smiling in an odd, pitiful way. He looked terrible – more ill than ever.

'There – I *have* come to see you,' he said in a thick voice, without taking his eyes off Levin's face. 'I've wanted to for a long time, but I never felt well. Now I'm much better.'

'Yes, yes!' answered Levin, shocked at the sight of him. And he felt even more frightened when his lips touched Nikolai's dry skin as they kissed, and he saw his brother's large eyes shining in an unnatural way.

'I'll stay with you for a month or two, then I'll go back to Moscow,' said Nikolai. 'I've been promised a position there. I've got so many new plans. I got rid of Maria – I need to make a fresh start. The important thing is to have one's health, and my health, thank God, has mended.'

Levin listened, but he could think of nothing to say. Then Nikolai began questioning him about his affairs, and Levin told him of his plans for the peasants. Nikolai listened, but it was clear he was not really interested.

At this moment both of them had only one thought – Nikolai's illness and approaching death. But neither of them dared speak of it, so everything else they spoke of seemed unnatural and false. Levin felt very glad when the evening was over and it was time to go to bed. He wanted to cry over his much-loved brother who was dying, but instead he had to listen to him talking about how he planned to live.

Levin's bedroom was the only one which was heated, so Levin put his brother's bed in there behind a screen. For a long time, he lay in bed listening to Nikolai coughing and thinking about death. Suddenly he remembered how they used to go to bed when they were children and throw pillows at each other and laugh helplessly, full of life and happiness.

'He's dying,' he thought. 'He'll be dead before the spring, and how can I help him? What can I say to him?'

If Nikolai and Levin could have spoken from the heart, they would have looked into each other's eyes, and Levin would have said, 'You're dying, you're dying!' and Nikolai would have replied, 'I know, but I'm afraid, I'm afraid!' This was in their hearts, but it was impossible for them to say it.

On the third day of his stay, Nikolai challenged his brother to explain his new plans once more, and when he did so, started to criticize them. This made Levin very angry.

'I'm trying to find a way of making work profitable for myself and the peasants,' said Levin. 'I want to organize . . .'

'You don't want to organize anything. You want to show that you're not simply using the peasants, but have new ideas.'

'If that's what you think . . . leave me alone!' said Levin.

'I certainly will! You can go to the devil! And I'm very sorry I ever came!'

In spite of all his efforts to make peace with his brother afterwards, Nikolai would not listen but insisted that it was better for him to leave. He had already packed his bags when Levin went to him and asked Nikolai to forgive him if he had hurt his feelings in any way.

'If you want to feel that you're right, I can give you that satisfaction,' said Nikolai, and smiled. 'You *are* right, but I'm going to leave anyway. Don't think too badly of me, Kostya, will you?' And his voice trembled.

These were the only sincere words that had passed between them. Levin understood that they were meant to say, 'You see, and you know, that I'm in a bad way, and perhaps we shall never see each other again.' Tears poured down from his eyes. He kissed his brother once more, but could not say anything.

A few days later, Levin went abroad to Europe.

Chapter 7   The Dinner Party

The Karenins continued living in the same house and met every day, so that the servants would not gossip. Vronsky never came to the Karenins' house, but Anna met him away from home, and her husband was aware of it.

The situation was a miserable one for all three. Each of them hoped that something would happen to change it, but none of them did anything to make change happen.

One day, Vronsky arrived home and found a note from Anna. 'I am ill and unhappy,' she wrote. 'I cannot go out, but I cannot go on any longer without seeing you. Come this evening. My husband will be at a meeting till ten.'

Vronsky lay down on the sofa and fell asleep. He had a very strange and unpleasant dream about Anna and an old peasant. The peasant – a dirty little man with a beard – was bending down and muttering strange words in French. Vronsky awoke in the dark, trembling with horror.

'What stupidity!' he thought and glanced at his watch. It was half-past eight already and he would have to hurry to get to Anna's before her husband came home. He rang for his servant, dressed and went out, completely forgetting his dream.

When he got to the Karenins' house, the servant who opened the door looked at him in surprise. Then Vronsky almost ran into Karenin in the doorway. Karenin stared at the visitor with steady, dull eyes, then pressed his lips together, lifted his hand to his hat and went out.

'If he fought me, I could do something,' Vronsky thought angrily. 'But he puts me in the position of a snake in the grass, which I never meant and never mean to be.'

He heard the sound of Anna's footsteps. She came and laid her hands on his shoulders, and gave him a long searching look, her eyes full of love.

'What was your husband doing here?' he asked. 'I thought he was at a meeting.'

'He was, but he came back early. Now he has to go out somewhere else,' she replied. 'But where have you been?'

Vronsky was invited to many parties and other events in Petersburg high society. Sometimes there were beautiful women at these events, and Anna got very jealous imagining him with them. Her jealousy filled Vronsky with horror, although he knew that her love for him was the cause of it.

He had often told himself that to be loved by Anna was happiness, but he was much further from happiness than when he had followed her from Moscow. Anna was not like the woman he had first fallen in love with. She was like a faded flower that a man has picked, in which it is difficult to find the beauty that first made him pick it and destroy it.

'Tell me about this illness of yours,' said Vronsky. 'What did the doctor say? Perhaps it is not illness at all, but is because of your condition. When is the baby going to come?'

A gentle sadness spread over Anna's face.

'Soon, soon. We shall soon all be at peace.'

She laid her lovely white hand on his sleeve, and her eyes filled with tears.

'I don't understand. What do you mean?' he asked.

'I'm going to die in childbirth,' she replied. 'I know it.'

Vronsky felt afraid, but he said, 'What nonsense you talk!'

'No, it's true,' said Anna. 'I had a dream about it. I dreamed that I ran into my bedroom, and in the corner was a horrible little old peasant man with a dirty beard. He was bending over something, and muttering strange things in French. I was so frightened that I tried to wake up, but I could not. Then I knew that I would die in childbirth.'

She looked at Vronsky with terror in her face. Vronsky, remembering his own dream, felt the same terror. But all he said was, 'What nonsense, what nonsense!'

Karenin was very angry about meeting Vronsky at his own door. He had made Anna promise only one thing – not to receive her lover in his house – and she had broken her promise. So now he must punish her and carry out his threat to divorce her and take his son away. In the morning, he went directly to Anna's room. He walked in without greeting her, and went straight to her writing table and unlocked it.

'What do you want?' she cried.

'Your lover's letters.' He opened a drawer where he knew she kept her most important papers, and took out a bundle of letters. Anna tried to stop him, but he pushed her away.

'Sit down!' he told her, putting the letters under his arm. 'I asked you not to have your lover in this house, but you did. I am going to Moscow. But first I will ask a lawyer to arrange a divorce. My son will go to my sister's.'

'You only want Seriozha in order to hurt me,' she said. 'You don't love him . . . Leave me Seriozha!'

'Yes, I have lost even my love for my son, because he reminds me of you. But I shall take him anyway. Goodbye!'

Anna took Karenin's hand and whispered, 'Leave me Seriozha! I have nothing else to say, but please leave me Seriozha until my . . . leave him with me!'

But Karenin pulled his hand away and left the room.

He went immediately to the offices of a very famous Petersburg lawyer. There was a crowd of people in the lawyer's waiting room, but the clerk took Karenin's card to the lawyer. A few moments later, the lawyer came out of his office.

'Please come in and sit down,' he said to Karenin. 'What can I do for you?'

Karenin looked at the lawyer's face, and saw that his clever grey eyes were laughing.

'He knows my situation already,' he thought. He hesitated, then began to speak. 'I am in an unhappy position,' he began. 'My wife has deceived me, and I wish to obtain a divorce, but I do not want my son to remain with his mother.'

'So you want me to tell you how you can get a divorce?' asked the lawyer. 'Very well. The most usual reasons for divorce are – if husband or wife has abandoned the other for five years, or if both partners agree that adultery has taken place.'

'I have letters here from my wife's lover which can prove her adultery,' said Karenin.

'Letters are not enough,' said the lawyer. 'Direct evidence is required – eye-witnesses. If you agree to use my services, it is best to let me arrange all that.'

'I see,' said Karenin, turning pale. 'Then, from what you say, a divorce is possible.'

'Quite possible. But you must allow me to act freely. When may I expect to hear from you?'

'In a week. I'll write and let you know what I decide.'

Karenin had to visit the distant provinces of Russia on business, and on his way there stopped for three days in Moscow.

The day after his arrival, he was driving back from a visit to the Governor-General when somebody called his name in a loud and cheerful voice. He saw Oblonsky standing on the pavement, looking young and happy and wearing a stylish overcoat and hat.

Karenin did not want to see anyone in Moscow, especially his wife's brother. But Oblonsky ran quickly across the snow.

'I'm so glad to see you. Why didn't you tell us you were in town? Listen, tomorrow we're having a dinner party. Please come. We'll expect you between five and six o'clock.'

The next day was Sunday. Oblonsky's latest girlfriend was a dancer, and he went first to the theatre to see her and give her a present of an expensive necklace. Then he went to the market and chose the fish and vegetables for the dinner party. He wanted to have only the very best food and drink there.

Levin was also in Moscow, on his way back from Europe. Oblonsky had invited Levin to dinner, and Kitty too. He loved giving dinner parties in his home. Only one thing troubled him – Karenin had been very cold when they had met in the street the day before. Oblonsky had heard the rumours about Anna and Vronsky, and he guessed that all was not well between Karenin and his sister.

He decided to go and see Karenin at his hotel. Karenin was in his room, just finishing a letter to the lawyer in Petersburg. He had told the lawyer to act as he thought best.

When Oblonsky came in, Karenin said at once, 'I can't come to dinner at your house tonight.'

'Why can't you?' said Oblonsky, opening wide his clear, bright eyes. 'You promised.'

'I am planning to divorce your sister, my wife. I ought to have . . .'

Before Karenin could finish his sentence, Oblonsky sank into a chair.

'No,' he said. 'I can't believe it. I know Anna – forgive me – she's a fine, splendid woman – and so I can't believe it. There must be some misunderstanding.'

'I only wish it were a misunderstanding!'

'This is terrible!' said Oblonsky. 'Before you make a final decision, please talk to my wife. She loves Anna like a sister, she loves you and she's a wonderful woman. Please come to dinner tonight.'

'All right. If you wish it so much, I will come.'

◆

The Oblonskys' dinner party was going well. At first the guests were shy and awkward with each other, and Karenin stood stiffly by himself with an icy expression on his face. But Oblonsky, who was an excellent host, introduced everybody and started some interesting subjects for discussion. Soon the whole room was filled with animated conversation.

Levin, too, was a guest. He had not spoken to Kitty since the evening at her parents' home when he had met Vronsky. He had heard she was coming to the Oblonskys' dinner party, and was conscious of great joy, but also great fear, at the thought of seeing her.

When he walked into the room, she looked scared and shy, and was therefore more charming. She, too, was filled with joy and confusion. He went up to her and bowed, and she smiled at him and pressed his hand, saying, 'What a long time it is since we met!'

'But I have seen you,' said Levin, smiling happily.

'Where?'

'In the carriage on the way to your country house,' Levin replied, ready to cry with the emotions flooding his heart.

Oblonsky had put Kitty and Levin next to each other at dinner. During the meal, they chatted easily with each other and Levin felt as if he had grown wings. He smiled happily at everybody, but the only person who existed for him at that dinner and in the whole world was Kitty.

The dinner was a great success, with perfect food and wine. The conversation flowed smoothly and towards the end became so animated that even Karenin became less frozen.

After dinner, Dolly went up to Karenin and said, 'I'm so glad you came. I must have a talk with you.'

She took him into a private room. Dolly was sure of Anna's innocence, and she felt herself growing pale and her lips trembling with anger at this cold, unfeeling man who was so calmly intending to ruin her innocent friend.

'I asked you at dinner about Anna,' she said, 'and you didn't answer me. Please tell me, what is wrong between you?'

'Your husband has told you the reason why I am going to divorce her?' replied Karenin.

'I don't believe it!' cried Dolly, putting her hands to her head and closing her eyes. 'You must have made a mistake.'

Karenin smiled coldly at this passionate defence of Anna.

'It is very difficult to make a mistake when a wife informs her husband that eight years of married life have all been an error, and that she wants to begin life again,' he said angrily. 'I wish I *had* made a mistake. When I was still not sure, I was miserable, but it was not so hard as it is now. I am very unhappy.'

Dolly looked into his suffering face and saw that he spoke the truth. Her faith in Anna's innocence began to grow weaker.

'Oh, this is awful, awful! But are you really determined to divorce her? She will be nobody's wife; she will be lost!'

'But what else can I do?' said Karenin. 'I cannot forgive her – I do not want to, and do not think it would be right. I have never hated anyone, but I hate her with all my soul because of all the wrong she has done me!'

After dinner, Kitty had gone into the sitting-room and sat down at a card-table. Levin followed her. Taking a piece of chalk, Kitty began drawing circles on the new green cloth.

'I've wanted to ask you a question for a long time,' said Levin softly, looking into her tender but frightened eyes.

'What is it?'

'Here,' he said, and wrote down the initial letters, W, y, t, m, *i, c, n, b* – d, t, m, n, o, t? These letters stood for 'When you told me *it could not be* – did that mean never, or then?'

She looked up at him seriously, then began to read.

'I know what it is,' she said, turning a little red.

'What is this word?' he asked, pointing to the *n* which stood for 'never'.

'That means "never",' she said, 'but it's not true!'

He quickly rubbed out what he had written, handed her the chalk and stood up. She wrote: T, I, c, n, a, d.

The sight of Levin and Kitty together made Dolly feel less miserable after her conversation with Karenin: Kitty sat with the chalk in her hand, looking up at Levin with a shy, happy smile, as his fine figure bent over the table, his shining eyes looking at her. He was full of joy; he had understood. The letters meant: 'Then I could not answer differently.'

He glanced at her questioningly.

'Only then?'

'Yes,' her smile answered.

'And now?'

'Well, read this! I'll tell you what I would like so much!' She wrote the initial letters: I, y, c, f, a, f, w, h, meaning 'If you could forget and forgive what happened.'

Levin took the chalk and with nervous, trembling fingers, wrote the first letters of the following sentence: 'I have nothing to forget and forgive; I have never ceased to love you.'

'I understand,' she said in a whisper.

He sat down and wrote a long sentence. She understood it all, and without asking if she was right, took the chalk and at once wrote the answer. Levin could not fill in the words she meant at all, but he saw everything he needed to know in her lovely eyes. He wrote down three more letters; she read them over his arm and wrote the answer, 'Yes'.

Chapter 8   A Difficult Birth

When Karenin returned to his lonely room, his servant brought him a telegram. It was from Anna.

'*I am dying. I beg you to come. I shall die easier with your forgiveness,*' he read.

'Is this a trick?' he thought to himself. 'But if she is really ill, and I refuse to see her, it would be cruel. I must go.'

He had known for some time that Anna was pregnant with Vronsky's child, and realized that it was time for the child's birth. He took the night train to Petersburg, and drove through the streets in the early morning mist before the shops were open. Part of him was hoping that she was dead, because he knew that her death would solve many problems.

Before Karenin could ring the bell, a servant opened it.

'How is my wife?'

'She had a baby daughter yesterday. But she is very ill. The doctor is here now.'

As Karenin passed through the hall, he noticed a military overcoat hanging on the hallstand.

'Who else is here?' he asked.

'Count Vronsky, sir.'

Karenin went upstairs. Vronsky was sitting in a low chair by her writing-table, with his face hidden in his hands. He jumped up, but when he saw Karenin he sat down again, his face covered with confusion.

'She is dying,' he said. 'The doctors say there is no hope. Please let me stay here . . .'

Karenin turned away. He could hear the sound of Anna's voice, speaking in high animated tones, and went into her bedroom. Anna was lying with her face towards him, with red cheeks and shining eyes.

'Why doesn't my husband come?' she was saying. 'He is a good man. You say he won't forgive me, because you do not know him. Oh, why doesn't he come?'

Suddenly she stopped talking. She had seen Karenin.

'No, no,' she began, 'I am not afraid of him, I am afraid of death. Alexei, come here. I am in a hurry, because I have not much longer to live. The fever will come back to me soon, and then I will understand nothing more.'

A look of deep suffering came over Karenin's face. He tried to say something but could not speak a word. He looked at her and saw her looking at him tenderly.

'Stay a little, stay!' she went on. 'This is what I wanted to say. There is another woman in me, I'm afraid of her; it was she who fell in love with that man. I'm not that woman. Now I'm my real self, all myself. I'm dying now, I know I am. I only want one thing – forgive me, forgive me completely!'

A warm feeling of love and forgiveness filled Karenin's heart. He knelt down and, laying his head in the curve of her arm, which burned like fire through her sleeve, he cried like a child. She put her arm round his head and moved closer to him.

'Remember one thing: that I only wanted your forgiveness, nothing more, nothing more ... Why doesn't *he* come?' she cried, turning to Vronsky at the door. 'Come in, come in! Give him your hand.'

Vronsky approached the side of the bed and, seeing Anna, buried his face in his hands again.

'Uncover your face!' she said. 'Alexei, uncover his face! I want to see him!'

Karenin gently took Vronsky's hands away from his face, terrible with its look of deep pain and shame.

'Give him your hand. Forgive him.'

Karenin held out his hand, not even attempting to stop the tears that flowed down his cheeks.

'Thank God, thank God!' cried Anna. 'Now everything is ready. Oh God, when will it end?'

The doctor said that Anna was suffering from a fever which in ninety-nine cases out of a hundred was fatal. Towards midnight she lay still and quiet, and the end was expected every moment. But the following day her condition was the same, and the doctor said there was hope.

Karenin went into the room where Vronsky was sitting and sat down opposite him.

'I had decided on a divorce because I had a desire for revenge on you and her,' he said. 'When I got her telegram, I came here with many feelings – I will say more, I hoped for her death. But . . . I saw her and forgave her. My duty is clear: I ought to remain with her, and I will. If she wants to see you, I will let you know, but now I think you had better go.'

Vronsky could not understand Karenin, but it seemed to him that there was something very noble about Karenin's actions. He went out on to the steps of the Karenins' house, feeling ashamed, humiliated and guilty. The husband, the deceived husband – who until now had appeared a pitiful object – had shown himself to be kind, honourable and a better man than Vronsky.

He went home and tried to sleep, but could not. Pictures and memories came into his mind; his happiest moments with Anna, and his recent humiliation. 'Take away his hands,' she had said, and he recalled the ridiculous look of shame on his face when Karenin took his hands away.

'Am I going mad?' he thought. 'Perhaps I am. I must think what to do. What is left?' He thought about his army career, Serpuhovsky and the Court, but it all seemed meaningless. He got up and began walking up and down the room. 'This is how people go mad,' he said again, 'and shoot themselves . . .'

He closed the door, went to the table and picked up his gun. For a minute or two he stood without moving, holding the gun in his hand as memories of lost happiness filled his mind. He put the gun to his heart and fired. He did not hear the shot, but felt a violent blow. Then he saw blood on the carpet and his hand, and realized he had tried to shoot himself.

'Fool! I missed!' he said, reaching again for the gun. Then he fell over and lay on the floor. A few minutes later his frightened servant, who had heard the noise of the gun, came in and ran to get help. Three doctors put Vronsky to bed.

◆

Karenin had forgiven his dying wife completely. He forgave Vronsky too and pitied him, especially after he heard that Vronsky had tried to shoot himself. He pitied his son, and felt sorry that he had not taken enough interest in him. But for the newborn baby girl he had a very strange feeling – not of pity, but of love. He would sit calmly by her bedside for hours, looking at the sleeping baby and feeling very peaceful.

As Anna got better, Karenin noticed that she was afraid of him, and uncomfortable in his presence. She could not look him straight in the face. One day in February, he returned home in the afternoon and found that she had a visitor – her friend, Princess Betsy, whom Karenin had never liked.

When Karenin entered Anna's bedroom, Betsy jumped up.

'I must go,' she said. 'Anna and I have been talking too much.'

'No, stay a moment, please,' said Anna. 'I have something to tell you,' she went on, turning to Karenin. 'I cannot have any secrets from you, nor do I wish to.

'Betsy tells me that Count Vronsky has accepted a post in Tashkent, in Central Asia. He wants to come and say goodbye to me before he goes, but I told him I could not see him.'

'I am very grateful to you for telling me . . .' Karenin began, but stopped, unable to discuss things in the presence of Princess Betsy. As Betsy left the room, Karenin followed her.

'I know you are a very good-hearted man,' said Princess Betsy, stopping and pressing Karenin's hand. 'Let Vronsky come. He is going away to Tashkent for a long time.'

'Thank you for your advice, Princess,' replied Karenin, 'but my wife can decide for herself whom she wants to see.'

When he returned to Anna's room, she looked at him nervously and he saw that she had been crying.

'I am very grateful for your decision,' he said. 'As Count Vronsky is going away, there is no need for him to come here.'

'No,' Anna thought, 'no need for a man to come and say goodbye to the woman he loves, for whom he was ready to ruin himself — has ruined himself. No need at all for him to say goodbye to the woman who cannot live without him!'

'Let us never speak of it,' she said calmly, but there was a look of hatred in her face.

As Betsy was leaving the Karenins' house, she met Oblonsky, who was in Petersburg for a few days, mainly because he was hoping to advance his career. Oblonsky greeted Betsy in his usual cheerful way and kissed her hand.

'I am glad you are here,' she said, adding in a whisper full of meaning, 'He will kill her. It's an impossible situation — he doesn't understand her feelings. The whole town is talking about it. He must either take her away or get a divorce.'

'Yes,' said Oblonsky. 'That's why I've come to Petersburg — to persuade Karenin to give her a divorce.'

He kissed Betsy's hand again and went in to see his sister. He asked her how she was and how she had spent the morning.

'Very, very miserably. Today and this morning and all other days, past and future,' she said.

'I know it's hard, but you must make an effort and look life in the face,' said Oblonsky cheerfully. 'Nothing is so very terrible.'

'No, Stiva,' said Anna, 'I'm lost, I'm lost. But it's not over yet . . . and the end will be terrible.'

'Listen to me,' said Oblonsky. 'You can't see your own position, but I can. You married a man older than yourself, and you married him without love. That was a mistake, admit it.'

'A terrible mistake!' said Anna.

'Then you had the bad luck to fall in love with a man who was not your husband. Your husband forgave you, but . . . can you go on living with him? Do you wish it? Does he wish it?'

'I don't know, I don't know at all.'

'You're miserable, he's miserable, and what good can come of it? But a divorce would solve everything. Let me try and arrange things. Don't say a word! I'm going to him now.'

Anna made no reply, but she looked at her brother with dreamy, shining eyes. Oblonsky walked into Karenin's study and found Karenin walking up and down.

'I'm not disturbing you?' said Oblonsky. 'I wanted to have a little talk with you about my sister.'

'I think of nothing else. And here is what I had begun to write, thinking that I could express it better in a letter,' replied Karenin. He showed Oblonsky the letter he had written.

I can see that my presence is disagreeable to you. As God is my witness, when I saw you at the time of your illness, I decided with my whole heart to forget about what had happened. My only desire was for the good of your soul, and now I see that I have not succeeded in saving that. Tell me what will make you happy and give you peace of mind; I place myself in your hands.

Oblonsky handed back the letter and continued looking at Karenin in wonder, not knowing what to say.

'I have to know what she wants,' said Karenin.

'Well,' replied Oblonsky, 'there is a way out of every situation. And both of you need to have your freedom.'

'You mean, divorce,' said Karenin.

'Yes, divorce,' replied Oblonsky. 'It is really very simple.'

Karenin made no reply. What seemed so simple to Oblonsky, he had considered thousands of times, and it seemed to him impossible. An action for divorce meant that his wife, whom he loved and had forgiven, would be put to shame. And what would happen to his son?

If he divorced Anna, she would join her life to Vronsky's. Their union would be both illegal and sinful because a wife, according to church law, could not marry again while her husband was living. 'In a year or two he will abandon her, or she will take a new lover,' he thought. 'And I, because I consented to a divorce, will be the cause of her ruin.'

'The only question is,' Oblonsky was saying, 'on what conditions are you prepared to consent to a divorce?'

'Oh God! How have I deserved this?' thought Karenin.

'All right, all right,' he cried in a loud voice, 'I will give her a divorce, I will even give up my son . . .'

And turning away, he sat down on a chair by the window.

'Alexei, believe me, she will appreciate your generosity,' said Oblonsky. 'I am doing my best to help both you and her.'

When he left Karenin's study, he felt very pleased with himself at having successfully arranged the matter; he felt certain that Karenin would not break his promise.

◆

Vronsky's wound was a dangerous one, although it had missed the heart, and for several days he lay between life and death. As the days passed and he got better, he firmly decided to give up Anna; but he could not tear out of his heart his sadness at the loss of her love.

Serpuhovsky arranged a post for him in Tashkent, and Vronsky accepted it gladly. Then Princess Betsy came to see him with the news, which she had heard through Oblonsky, that Karenin had consented to a divorce, and that therefore there was nothing to stop him from seeing Anna.

Vronsky drove straight to the Karenins. He ran up the steps and entered Anna's room. Without looking round to see if they were alone, he began showering her face, neck and hands with kisses. Anna tried to calm him, but it was too late. Her lips trembled and for a long time she could not speak.

'We shall be so happy,' he said. 'We'll go to Italy; you will soon get well.'

'Is it really possible that we could be like husband and wife, alone together, with our own family?' she said. 'Stiva says my husband has consented to everything, but I don't know what he will finally decide about Seriozha.'

'Don't talk about that now, don't think of it,' he said.

'Oh, why did I not die? It would have been better,' she said, and the tears streamed silently down her cheeks.

At one time Vronsky would have thought it disgraceful and impossible to refuse a post at Tashkent, but he did so now without hesitation. Then he resigned from the army.

A month later, Karenin was left alone in the house with his son, and Anna went abroad with Vronsky and their baby daughter. She had still not obtained a divorce.

Chapter 9   Home and Away

Vronsky and Anna travelled in Europe for three months, and at last settled in a small Italian town.

Anna, in this first period of her freedom and rapid return to health, was full of the joys of life. The thought of her husband's suffering did not poison her own happiness. The more she got to know Vronsky, the more she loved him. She loved him for himself, and for his love for her. To have him all to herself was a continual joy, his presence always a delight. Separation from the son she loved – even that did not cause her pain at first. The baby girl, Ani, was so sweet, and Anna had grown so fond of her, that she rarely thought of Seriozha.

Vronsky, however, was not entirely happy. For a time after leaving the army and uniting his life with Anna's, he too experienced all the joys of freedom. He was content, but not for long. Sixteen hours of the day must be filled somehow and, cut off from the social life he had enjoyed in Petersburg, he tried to find new interests – first politics, then new books, then pictures. He settled down to work at painting, and began to paint a portrait of Anna in Italian costume.

He also painted a picture of the attractive Italian nurse who looked after the baby. This nurse was a secret shadow in Anna's life. Vronsky admired her beauty, and Anna dared not confess to herself that she was becoming jealous.

But Vronsky's interest in painting did not last long. Without an occupation, both his life and Anna's seemed very dull and boring in the little Italian town. They decided to go back to Russia and spend the summer on Vronsky's large family estate in the country. But first they planned to spend a few days in Petersburg, where Anna was hoping to see her son.

◆

Levin and Kitty got married. They had a big traditional wedding ceremony in Moscow with many guests. Levin was in a continual state of happiness – everything was like a dream. He let Oblonsky and Kitty's family make all the arrangements for the wedding, and agreed to everything that was suggested.

After the wedding, Kitty wanted to go straight to Levin's country estate. She knew Levin loved his work there, and that it was very important to him.

Levin was very happy with married life, although it was not as easy as he had imagined it. He felt like a man who, after admiring the smooth motion of a boat on the water, suddenly finds himself in the boat with deep water all around. He had to work hard to guide the boat safely through the water, and this work was very difficult at times, although delightful.

After they had been married about three months, Levin received a letter from Maria, the woman who had previously lived with his brother Nikolai in Moscow. She wrote that she was with Nikolai again, but that he was dying.

'I must go to him at once,' said Levin.

'Then I'll come with you,' replied Kitty.

'No, Kitty,' he said. 'That's impossible.'

'What do you mean?' she asked, hurt that he was not pleased by her suggestion. 'Why can't I come?'

'Well, that woman will be there. I don't want you to have contact with her.'

'I don't care about her. All I know is that my husband's brother is dying, and my husband is going to him, and that I am going with my husband.'

In the end Kitty won the argument, and they started for Moscow together on the following day.

Nikolai and Maria were staying at an inn that was very small and dirty. When Maria heard of Levin and Kitty's arrival, she came at once. She was just the same as when Levin had seen her in Moscow – she was wearing the same old woollen dress, and had the same good-natured but stupid expression on her face.

'How is he?' asked Levin.

'Very bad. He has been expecting you all the time.'

When Maria saw Kitty, her face turned red and her eyes filled with tears. But Kitty was not embarrassed; she looked at Maria with an eager curiosity.

Levin left Kitty in their room and went to see his brother. The room where Nikolai was lying was dirty and evil-smelling. On a bed in the corner lay a body covered by a blanket. Huge wrists attached to horribly thin arms hung out from under the blanket. The head lay sideways on the pillow and the thin hair was wet with sweat. Levin was shocked.

'It can't be that this awful body is my brother Nikolai?' he thought. But as he went closer, he saw that in spite of the terrible changes in the body and face, it was his living brother. He took Nikolai's hand, and Nikolai smiled.

'You did not expect to find me like this,' he said, speaking with difficulty.

'No,' said Levin.

Levin had not wanted Kitty to see Nikolai, because he thought she would be upset. But Kitty suddenly came into the room, and went straight to Nikolai and took his hand. She was filled with pity for the sick man, and started at once to find ways of making him more comfortable. She sent for the doctor, found a servant to clean the room and washed Nikolai's blankets herself. Soon Nikolai, washed and with his hair combed, was sitting up in bed with a new expression of hope.

'I feel much better already,' he said, taking Kitty's hand and raising it to his lips. 'With you I would have got better long ago. How nice it feels! Now turn me over on my left side,' he whispered to Levin. 'I want to sleep.'

It was terrible for Levin to put his arms round that awful body, but he managed to turn his brother over. Nikolai pulled at his hand and kissed it. Levin's eyes were full of tears and, without saying a word, he left the room.

The next day, Nikolai seemed much better. He sat up, coughed only a little, had some soup and talked, so that Levin and Kitty began to feel optimistic that he might recover. But by the evening he was worse and Maria came to tell them he was dying. They both ran to his room.

'I feel I'm going,' said Nikolai. But he did not die at once. He lay in the same condition for ten days, suffering terrible pain.

Sometimes he would cry out, 'Oh, when will this end? When will it be over?' He could not lie comfortably in any position. He only wanted his suffering to be over – to be dead.

On the tenth day after Levin and Kitty's arrival, Kitty was ill. She had a headache, was sick and could not leave her bed in the morning. The doctor said she was tired and should rest.

After dinner, however, she got up and went to Nikolai.

'How do you feel?' she asked him.

'Worse,' he replied. 'The pain is terrible.'

'The end will come today, you'll see,' whispered Maria. Kitty sent for the priest to come and read the prayers for the dying. Before he had finished, the dying man opened his eyes. The priest put the cross to Nikolai's cold forehead, then stood silent and touched the huge, bloodless hand that was turning cold. Nikolai was dead.

The sight of his much-loved brother, and the presence of death, was terrible for Levin, but now, because his wife was there, he did not feel despair. And the mystery of death had only just passed before his eyes when another mystery called him back to life and love. The doctor told them that Kitty's sickness was due to pregnancy.

◆

Karenin was deeply unhappy. He could not understand how, after forgiving his wife, he now found himself alone. He was sure that everyone was laughing at his humiliating position.

For the first two days after Anna had left, he had tried to appear calm, and nobody could have guessed that he was in despair. But on the third day, when a hat-maker brought him a bill that Anna had forgotten to pay, he could not hide his emotion any longer. He sat down at the table, with his head in his hands and unable to speak. His despair was made worse because he did not have anyone to talk to about his problems. Although he knew a lot of people, he had not one real friend.

But there was one person in Petersburg who had not forgotten Karenin. This was the Countess Lydia Ivanovna. At the bitterest moment of his lonely despair, she arrived at the house and walked straight into his study. She found him as he was sitting with his head in both hands.

'I have heard everything!' she cried, taking his hand in hers and looking into his eyes. 'My dear friend!' she said again, looking as if she was going to cry. 'Your sorrow is great, but you must not let it overcome you.'

'I am weak, broken and completely crushed!' said Karenin. 'And the worst thing is that I can find no support anywhere, not even in myself.'

'You will find support,' she said. 'Seek it – not in me, although I beg you to believe in my friendship. Our support is love, the love that God has given to us. He will be your support and help.' The Countess was a keen follower of a new kind of religious teaching that had recently spread in Petersburg.

'It's not the loss of what no longer exists,' continued Karenin. 'That does not cause me sorrow. But I feel humiliated in front of other people at the position I am in.

'In my lonely situation I have to spend the whole day making arrangements about household matters – the servants, the teacher, the bills. I have not the strength to bear it.'

'I understand, my dear friend,' said the Countess Lydia Ivanovna. 'I see a woman's word, a woman's guiding hand are needed here. Will you trust me?'

Silently and gratefully, Karenin pressed her hand.

'I will help you – I will be your housekeeper. And we will take care of Seriozha together. No, don't thank me. Thank Him, and ask His help, for in Him alone we find peace, comfort and love,' she said, raising her eyes to Heaven.

Karenin listened to her, and although he had once disliked these open expressions of religion, now they seemed quite natural and gave him comfort.

'I am very, very grateful to you,' he said.

The Countess pressed his hands again.

'Now I must start work,' she said with a smile. 'I am going to Seriozha. I will not trouble you unless I have to.' She got up and went to Seriozha's part of the house. There, wetting the frightened boy's cheeks with her tears, she told him that his father was a saint and his mother was dead.

Chapter 10   Mother and Son

The Countess Lydia Ivanovna, when quite a young girl, had been married, but her husband had left her less than two months after the wedding. Since then, she had been in love with all sorts of people, but not in the same way that she was now in love with Karenin. She loved his soul, his high voice, his tired eyes, his character and his soft white hands.

One day, the Countess heard some most unwelcome news: Anna and Vronsky were in Petersburg. Immediately, she thought that Karenin must be saved from seeing that awful woman; he must not even find out that she was in the same town.

The next day, Lydia Ivanovna received a note and with horror recognized Anna's handwriting. It was brought by a man from the hotel where Anna was staying.

> *My dear Countess — I am very unhappy at being apart from my son and would very much like to see him before I leave Petersburg. I write to you and not to my husband simply because I do not wish to make that great-hearted man suffer in remembering me. Knowing your friendship for him, I am sure you will understand me. Will you send Seriozha to me, or should I come to the house at a fixed time? I know that you will not refuse me. You cannot imagine how much I desire to see my son, or how grateful I will be to you for this. Anna.*

Everything about the letter annoyed the Countess. She immediately wrote a note to Karenin, asking him to come and see her at her house about a serious and painful matter. When Karenin arrived, she made him some tea and showed him Anna's letter. He sat for a long time in silence.

Then he said, 'I do not think I have the right to refuse her.'

'My dear friend, you never see evil in anyone!'

'But I have forgiven her,' said Karenin, 'and so I cannot refuse her what her love − her love for her son − '

'But is it love, my friend? Is it sincere? Let us admit that you have forgiven her, but do we have the right to play with the feelings of that dear little boy? He thinks that she is dead. He prays for her. But what will he think if he sees her?'

'I had not thought of that,' said Karenin.

'If you ask my advice,' said the Countess, 'I advise you not to do it. It can only lead to further suffering for yourself and the child. With your permission I will write to her.'

Karenin consented, and the Countess wrote to Anna.

Madame − To remind your son of you might lead to questions on his part which would be very difficult to answer. It is therefore better for him not to see you.
May God have mercy on you. Countess Lydia.

This letter achieved the secret purpose which the Countess hid even from herself. It hurt Anna deeply. Her main reason for coming back to Russia had been to see her son, and she had not stopped to ask herself how it could be arranged. But as soon as she arrived in Petersburg, she suddenly realized her difficult position in society and understood that it would not be easy to arrange this meeting.

She did not discuss her feelings about Seriozha with Vronsky because she knew her son was not important to him. He could never understand the depth of her suffering, and if the subject was mentioned, would speak in a very cool tone.

When she received Countess Lydia's cruel and unexpected reply to her note, she was very hurt and angry.

'That coldness, that pretence of feeling!' she said to herself. 'They only want to hurt me and Seriozha.' And Anna decided that the next day, which was Seriozha's birthday, she would go straight to her husband's house and see her son, and destroy the lies they had surrounded him with.

She drove to a toyshop, bought a lot of toys and made a plan of action. She would go early in the morning, at about eight o'clock, before Karenin got up. She would give money to the servants so that they would let her in.

Seriozha was feeling excited about his birthday. The day before, he had gone out for a walk by himself. One of his favourite occupations was to look out for his mother during his walks. He did not believe she was dead, in spite of what the Countess Lydia Ivanovna had told him. Every attractive, graceful woman with dark hair was his mother, and at the sight of every such woman his heart swelled with tenderness and the tears came into his eyes.

The night before his birthday, when Seriozha was in bed, he prayed that tomorrow, for his birthday, his mother might stop hiding herself and come to him.

The next morning at eight o'clock, Anna rang the bell of the house where she had lived for nine years. An old servant of Karenin's answered it, and Anna put some money into his hand and walked past him into the hall. The old servant bowed in silence. With light steps Anna ran up the stairs and opened the door to her son's bedroom. Seriozha had just woken up.

'Seriozha!' she whispered, walking softly up to his bed.

How much he had changed since she left him; how much taller and thinner he had grown! Oh, how thin his face looked, and how short his hair was! How long his arms seemed! But it was still her Seriozha – there was the shape of his head, his lips, his soft neck and broad little shoulders.

He raised himself on his elbow, turned his head from side to side and opened his eyes. He stared questioningly for several seconds at his mother standing in front of him; then suddenly, he smiled happily and fell forward into her arms.

'Seriozha, my darling boy!' she whispered, putting her arms round his little body.

'Mama!' he said. Smiling sleepily, with his eyes still shut, he threw his arms round her shoulders and moved against her, rubbing his face against her neck.

'I knew,' he said, opening his eyes. 'Today is my birthday. I knew you'd come. I'll get up now . . .'

Anna watched him with hungry eyes and passed her hand over his head; she could not speak for tears.

'Why are you crying, Mama?' he said, completely awake now. 'Mama, why are you crying?' he asked in a tearful voice.

'I'm crying for joy! It's such a long time since I've seen you. But I won't cry any more. Come, it's time for you to get dressed,' she added and, never letting go of his hands, she sat down on the chair beside the bed where his clothes were lying ready for him. 'How do you get dressed without me?' She wanted to talk to him naturally and cheerfully, but could not.

'You're sitting on my clothes!' Seriozha began to laugh, and Anna smiled. He threw himself on her again. 'Mama, dearest Mama!' And then he started kissing her again.

'You didn't think I was dead, did you?'

'I never believed it. I knew! I knew!' he repeated.

Meanwhile, the old servant had gone downstairs and told the other servants that Anna had arrived unexpectedly and was now with Seriozha. They were worried because they knew it was Karenin's habit to go to Seriozha's room every morning.

Seriozha's old nurse went upstairs. When she entered the room, Seriozha was telling Anna excitedly about the time when he and a friend had fallen down a hill. Anna was listening to the sound of his voice and watching his face, but her only thought was that she must go, she must leave him.

'Dear Madam!' said the nurse, going up to Anna. 'God has brought joy to our birthday-boy! And you haven't changed one bit.' The nurse suddenly burst into tears and began kissing Anna's hand. Seriozha, smiling with joy, held his mother by one hand and his nurse by the other.

But the nurse was whispering something to his mother, and on his mother's face Seriozha saw an expression of fear and shame. She went up to him.

'My darling!' she said. She could not say 'goodbye', but the expression on her face said it, and he understood. 'You won't forget me? You ...' but she could say no more.

How many times afterwards did she think of all the things she might have said! But Seriozha understood everything. He understood that she was unhappy, and that she loved him. He understood that his father was coming to his room, and that he and his mother must not meet. But he could not understand why, when she had not done anything wrong, she looked afraid and ashamed. He held her in silence, and whispered, 'Don't go away. He won't come yet.'

'Seriozha, my darling,' Anna said. 'You must love him. He's better and kinder than I am, and I have been wicked to him. When you are grown up, you will understand.'

'No one is better than you!' he cried in despair.

'My little one!' said Anna, starting to cry.

At that moment the door opened and Karenin came in. Seriozha sank back on the bed and began to cry too, hiding his face in his hands. Anna moved his hands, once more kissed his wet face and then walked quickly towards the door. Karenin stopped and bowed his head.

Although she had just told Seriozha that Karenin was better and kinder than she, she was seized by a strong feeling of hatred for him and jealousy over her son. She hurriedly pulled her coat round her, and almost ran out of the room.

Anna had never imagined that seeing Seriozha would affect her so violently. When she returned to her lonely rooms at the hotel, it was a long time before she could remember why she was there. 'Yes, it's all over, and I am alone again,' she thought.

The Italian nurse came in with the baby, whom she had just dressed, and held her out to Anna. Anna took her in her arms, danced her up and down on her knee and kissed her, but there was no comparison between the feeling she had for this child and the love she felt for Seriozha. Everything about the baby was sweet, but for some reason she did not grip Anna's heart. All Anna's love was concentrated on Seriozha now, although he was the son of a man she did not love. And she was forever separated from him, not only physically but spiritually.

She gave the baby back to the nurse, and took out a book in which there were photographs of Seriozha at different ages. Next to one of the pictures was a photograph of Vronsky in Rome. She had not thought of him all morning but, seeing his photograph, felt a sudden rush of love for him.

'But where is he? How can he leave me alone in my unhappiness?' she thought, completely forgetting that she herself had not told Vronsky anything about her visit to her son. She sent a message asking him to come to her immediately. The servant returned with the answer that Count Vronsky had a visitor, Prince Yashvin, who had just arrived in Petersburg; he would come at once, and would bring Yashvin with him.

'He's not coming alone, so I can't tell him everything,' thought Anna. Suddenly a strange idea crossed her mind: had he ceased to love her? Was he trying to avoid being alone with her? 'If he doesn't love me any more, he should tell me,' thought Anna in despair.

But when Vronsky and Yashvin arrived, Anna was very pleasant and charming to them both. During the conversation, they talked about their plans for the evening. Yashvin told Anna there was a new opera singer in town, and all the most important people in Petersburg society were going to hear her.

After dinner that evening, Anna went to her room. When Vronsky went to see her a few minutes later, he found Anna wearing a beautiful dress that she had had made in Paris.

'What are you doing?' he asked.

'I'm going to the opera,' she replied.

'You know you can't go.'

'Why not?'

'Because if you show yourself there publicly, everybody will gossip about you and you will be humiliated.'

'I don't care!' Anna cried. 'For us, there is only one thing that matters – whether we love each other. We don't need to consider other people. Why can't I go out? I love you.'

For the first time, Vronsky experienced a feeling of anger, almost of hate, for Anna for her refusal to realize her position.

But later, when a servant had come to tell Vronsky that Anna had left the hotel, Vronsky decided he could not stay at home alone. Finally, he went to the theatre where the opera was being performed. The first act had already started. He looked around, but could not see Anna.

When the first act was over, Vronsky at last saw Anna's proud and lovely head. She was sitting with Prince Yashvin and a woman friend of hers. Her animated beauty and the brilliance of her eyes reminded him of her as he had seen her at the ball in Moscow. But he felt quite different about her beauty now; it still attracted him, but it held no mystery for him.

There was a couple on Anna's left whom Anna knew. The husband leaned across and began talking to Anna. Suddenly Vronsky saw the wife, a thin little woman, stand up, put on her coat and leave. Her face looked pale and angry, and she was speaking excitedly. Her husband looked anxiously at Anna, then followed his wife.

Everybody in the theatre had seen the incident. Vronsky did not know exactly what had passed between Anna and the couple, but he realized that something humiliating for Anna had happened. Then he saw his mother, with her steel-grey curls, and went up to her.

'I have been expecting you all evening, Alexei,' she said.

'I was just coming to see you, mother,' he said coldly.

'Why aren't you paying attention to Madame Karenina?' she asked. 'People are talking about her more than the opera.'

'I have asked you not to speak of that subject,' he said.

'I am only saying what everyone is saying.'

Vronsky made no reply but hurried straight to Anna's seat. He was angry with her for having put herself and him in a false position, but he also felt great pity for her suffering.

'You got here late, I think, and missed the best part,' she said. Suddenly her lovely face began to tremble, and she rose and left the theatre. Vronsky went back to his seat, but after a few minutes decided to follow Anna back to the hotel.

She was already there. When he entered, she was still in the same dress she had worn at the theatre. She was sitting in an armchair by the wall, staring straight in front of her.

'It's all your fault, all your fault!' she cried, tears of despair and anger in her voice.

'But I begged you not to go! I knew it would be unpleasant.'

'Unpleasant!' she cried. 'It was awful! I'll never forget it as long as I live. She said it was a disgrace to sit beside me.'

'A silly woman's talk,' he said. 'But why risk it?'

'If you loved me as I love you, if you were tortured as I am . . .' she said, looking at him with an expression of terror.

He was sorry for her, but angry too. He assured her of his love because he saw that this was the only way of calming her. She drank in his assurances of love eagerly, and gradually became quiet. The next day, fully at peace with one another, they left for the country.

Chapter 11   A Different World

Dolly and her children were spending the summer with Levin and Kitty at their country house. Oblonsky greatly approved of this arrangement. He said he was very sorry his official duties prevented him from passing the summer in the country with his family. He remained in Moscow, from time to time visiting them for a day or two.

Vronsky's country estate was only about eighty kilometres from the Levins, and Dolly decided that she would go and see Anna. She knew that Levin and Kitty did not want to meet Vronsky; but she felt she must go and see Anna, and show Anna that her feelings had not changed towards her.

She set out in a carriage before daybreak. The road was good, the carriage comfortable, and the peasant women whom she saw on the road waved to her cheerfully.

'Everyone seems to be enjoying life,' she thought to herself. 'These peasant women, and Kitty, and Anna – all of them, but not I. And everybody criticizes Anna. What for? Am I better than she is? She never loved her husband, but how can she be blamed for that? Very likely I would have done the same thing as her. But I don't know whether I should have listened to her when she came to me in Moscow. I ought to have left my husband then, and started again.'

When Anna saw her old friend Dolly approaching in her carriage, her face lit up with joy.

'I thought it was you, but didn't dare believe it! You can't imagine how glad I am!' she cried, pressing her face to Dolly's and kissing her. 'Here's a lovely surprise, Alexei!' she said to Vronsky.

'You have no idea how pleased we are to see you,' he said, showing his strong white teeth in a smile.

Anna took Dolly to her room, talking excitedly.

'You wonder how I can be happy in my position. Well, I'm ashamed to confess it, but . . . I *am* very happy. Something magical has happened to me; like when you wake up suddenly after a horrible, frightening dream and find that your terrors are over. Since we came here, I've been so happy!'

'I'm so glad!' said Dolly, returning Anna's smile. 'But why haven't you written to me?'

'I didn't know what you would think of me.'

'I don't think anything,' said Dolly. 'I've always loved you, and if one loves anyone, one loves the whole person, just as they are and not as one would like them to be.'

As Dolly said this, she saw that Anna had tears in her eyes. She pressed Anna's hand in silence.

The room where Anna took Dolly had more luxury than Dolly had ever known, luxury which reminded her of the best hotels abroad. When Anna had gone, Dolly looked round the room with the expert eye of a housewife. Everything was new, from the French wallpaper to the carpet which covered the whole floor.

When Anna came back, she had changed into a very simple dress. Dolly looked at it, knowing that, although it looked simple, it was very expensive.

'Well, Anna, and how is your little girl?' asked Dolly.

'Ani?' said Anna. 'Very well. Would you like to see her? Let's go to the nursery and I'll show her to you. She's very sweet; she can crawl now.'

There was just as much luxury in the nursery as in the rest of the house. There were expensive toys from England, and special furniture and baths for babies. The room itself was large, light and airy.

When they entered, the baby was just having her dinner. A Russian nurse was feeding the child and eating at the same time. Hearing Anna's voice, a tall, smart English nurse with an unpleasant face came in from the next room. To every word of Anna's, the nurse said, 'Yes, my lady.'

The pink-faced little girl with her black hair won Dolly's heart. She admired the way the baby crawled by supporting herself on her little hands and pushing forwards; not one of Dolly's own children had crawled like that. When Ani was put on the carpet she looked wonderfully sweet, looking round with bright black eyes, like a little wild animal, and smiling.

But Dolly did not like at all the general atmosphere of the nursery, and especially the English nurse. How could Anna have employed such an unpleasant-looking woman? The only explanation Dolly could think of was that no respectable nurse would have worked in Anna's household. Moreover, Dolly immediately realized that Anna's visit to the nursery was an unusual event. Anna wanted to get the baby one of her toys, but did not know where to look for it. Most surprising of all, when Dolly asked her how many teeth the child had, Anna made a mistake and knew nothing of the two latest teeth.

Later, Vronsky took Dolly for a walk in the garden. She had never really liked Vronsky; she had always thought him proud, and saw nothing in him of which he could be proud except his wealth. But here in his own house, he impressed her. She tried to find something to talk about and, because she could not think of anything else, told him how much she admired his house and garden. Vronsky had made many improvements to the house, and he was very pleased by Dolly's praise.

'Would you like to see the hospital?' he said. 'It's quite near.'

Vronsky was building a hospital for the peasants. He was very interested in this project and spent a lot of time on it. They walked out of the garden through a little gate, and Dolly saw before her a large red, nearly completed building. The iron roof, not yet painted, shone brightly in the sunshine, and there were busy workmen all around.

'It will all be ready by autumn,' Vronsky told Dolly. 'They've nearly finished inside.'

Vronsky led her inside the hospital, and showed her all the rooms. The walls were painted and the windows were already in; only the floors were not yet finished. They walked down the corridors and went through all the rooms where the patients would be, and Vronsky showed her the modern baths and beds.

Dolly was interested in and charmed by everything, and especially by Vronsky himself. 'Yes, he's a very nice, kind man,' she thought, not listening to what he was saying but watching him, while she mentally put herself in Anna's place. He was so eager and she liked him so much now that she began to understand how Anna could be in love with him.

After they had seen the hospital, they went back to the house. Dolly saw by Vronsky's face that there was something he wanted from her. As they walked back into the garden he said, 'You guess that I have something I want to say to you?'

Dolly felt afraid. What was he going to ask her? Did he want her to find a circle of friends for Anna in Moscow? Did he want her to bring her children to stay with them? Or did he want to tell her that he felt guilty about Kitty?

But Vronsky wanted to talk about none of these things.

'I know that I must be blamed for Anna's position,' he said, 'and I feel that very deeply.'

'I can see that Anna is very happy here with you; she's already told me so,' said Dolly, smiling. And as she said this, a doubt entered her mind; *was* Anna really happy?

'Yes, she's happy,' said Vronsky. 'But can it last? Whether we have acted rightly or wrongly is another question, and we are joined together for life. We have a child, we may have other children. But my daughter is by law not my daughter, but Karenin's. I cannot bear this false position!

'One day we may have a son, and by law he too would be a Karenin. However happy we may be in our home life here, or however many children we may have, there will be no legal tie between us. They will be Karenins. I have tried to talk to Anna about this, but she doesn't understand.

'I am happy in her love, but I must have an occupation too. Well, I have found an occupation and am proud of what I am doing. I love my work here with the hospital, and I want to know that what I do will not die with me. But my children will not be my own – they will belong to someone who hates them and will never see them!'

'Yes, I understand. But what can Anna do?' asked Dolly.

'Anna could . . . it depends on her . . . a divorce is essential,' he said. 'Karenin consented to a divorce – at that time your husband had almost arranged it – and I feel certain he would not refuse now if Anna asked him. Help me to persuade her to write to him and ask him for a divorce.'

'Of course I will,' said Dolly thoughtfully, remembering her last meeting with Karenin. 'I will talk to her.'

Anna was changing her dress for dinner – this was the third dress that Dolly had seen her in that day. Dolly felt like laughing because she had nothing to change into; she was already wearing her best dress.

The dinner, the dining room, the service, the wine and food were all excellent, and had the same feeling of luxury as the rest of the house. An architect and a few other local people had been invited, too. But Dolly noticed that Vronsky organized everything, and that Anna was more like a guest than a hostess.

As Dolly was getting ready for bed, Anna came to see her.

'How's Kitty?' she asked with a guilty glance. 'Is she still angry with me? Levin is a very nice man, they say.'

'Angry? Oh no,' replied Dolly, smiling. 'And Levin is much more than very nice. I don't know a better man.'

'Oh, I'm so glad,' said Anna.

'Now tell me about yourself. I've had a talk with . . .'

'With Alexei. I know you have. What did he say to you?'

'He spoke of something I wanted to ask you myself, so it is easy for me to speak for him – whether . . . whether you could not . . . put things right and improve your position.'

'You mean a divorce?' said Anna.

'Yes. He said that he wants you to be his. He does not want your husband to have a legal right to his children.'

'What children?' said Anna, half closing her eyes and not looking at Dolly.

'Ani, and others that will come.'

'There will be no more children. I don't wish it. I decided that after my illness and I'm doing something about it. I can choose either to be pregnant, or to be the friend and companion of my husband,' said Anna.

Dolly was shocked. She thought of all the families she knew with only one or two children and suddenly, for the first time, she understood this was by choice.

'But surely that's not right!' she said.

'But, Dolly, I'm not in the same position as you. There's a big difference between us. Don't you see that I could not possibly want children in my position?'

Dolly was silent. She suddenly felt an immense gap between her and Anna.

'Then that's one reason why you should get a divorce,' she said. 'Stiva told me your husband had consented.'

'Dolly, I don't want to talk about that.'

'All right,' said Dolly quickly, noticing the look of suffering on Anna's face. 'I just think that you look at the dark side of things too much.'

'Listen, Dolly. What can I do? You tell me to obtain a divorce. Don't you know how often I think about that! Not a day, not an hour passes without me thinking of it. It drives me mad! I can't get to sleep at night without morphine.

'But in the first place, *he* would never consent to a divorce now. He's under the influence of Countess Lydia Ivanovna. And if I receive his consent, what about my son? They will never let me have him. And so he will grow up, hating me, in the house of his father, whom I have abandoned.

'I love . . . equally, I think, but more than myself, two beings – Seriozha and Alexei. I love only these two beings, and one excludes the other. I cannot have them both; but that is my one need. And since I can't have that, I don't care about the rest. Nothing matters; nothing, nothing!'

When Dolly was left alone, she said her prayers and got into bed. She pitied Anna with all her heart. The thought of her own home and children acquired a new charm, and so sweet and precious did her little world seem that she did not want to stay away another day, and decided to go back to the Levins.

The next morning, as Dolly got ready for her journey home, Anna was sad. She knew that the feelings which Dolly's visit had awakened in her would never be stirred again. Those feelings were painful but they belonged to the better part of herself, which was being destroyed.

Dolly felt a great relief when they reached the open country. At the Levins' house, everybody was very pleased to see her. She gave them an animated description of her visit, and the luxury and good taste at Vronsky's house, and would not hear a word said against Anna.

Chapter 12   Jealousy

Vronsky and Anna went on living in the same way in the country all that summer and part of the autumn, still taking no steps to obtain a divorce.

One would have said that their life could not be improved on: they had enough money, good health, a child and plenty to occupy them both. Anna spent much of her time reading, both novels and serious literature. She made a special study, from books and technical journals, of every subject of interest to Vronsky. The hospital, too, interested her. She not only assisted there, but arranged and thought of many things herself.

Vronsky appreciated Anna's desire not only to please but to serve him, which had become the only aim of her existence. But at the same time he wanted to escape from the loving net in which she held him, and which put limits on his freedom.

In October there were important elections in the province of Kashin, where the estates of Vronsky, Levin and Oblonsky were. A friend of Vronsky's was a candidate in the elections, and Vronsky wanted to go and support him. Preparing himself for a quarrel with Anna, he told her coldly that he planned to go away for a few days. But to his surprise, Anna accepted the news calmly and only asked when he would return.

'I hope you won't be bored?' he said.

'I hope not,' said Anna. 'A box of books came for me yesterday. No, I shan't be bored.'

Vronsky was aware that she was not giving him a true explanation of her feelings, but he was very anxious to avoid a quarrel so he accepted what she said and left for the elections.

In September, Levin and Kitty had moved to Moscow to prepare for the birth of Kitty's baby. Levin had already spent a whole month there with nothing to do. Kitty, who saw that he was getting tired of Moscow, urged him to go to the elections, and as he also had some important business in Kashin, he went. Oblonsky was there, too.

These elections lasted for six days and were a good opportunity for men who had not seen each other for a long time to discuss politics and business matters.

Levin was aware of Vronsky's presence. At first he tried to avoid him, but this was impossible. One day Vronsky was standing with Oblonsky, and looked straight at Levin.

'I'm delighted to see you! I believe I've had the pleasure of meeting you . . . at Princess Shcherbatskaya's,' he said.

'Yes, I remember our meeting very well,' replied Levin, turning red and moving away. Vronsky smiled slightly and started talking to Oblonsky again.

On the last evening, there was a dinner to celebrate the election of the successful candidates. Vronsky, who had found the process of great interest and even had plans to offer himself as a candidate in the future, attended the dinner. The meal was excellent and very enjoyable, and afterwards the local governor invited Vronsky to a concert, followed by a ball.

'You'll see our local beauty there!' he said. Vronsky smiled, and promised to come.

They had all begun smoking, and were preparing to rise from the table when Vronsky's servant brought him a letter.

'This has come by special messenger,' he said.

The letter was from Anna, and even before he opened it he knew its contents. Thinking that the elections would take five days, he had promised to be back by Friday. It was now Saturday, and he knew the letter would be full of blame that he had not returned. He had sent a note to her the previous evening, but she had probably not received it yet. He opened the letter, and frowned as he read it.

'Ani is very ill. The doctor says it may be serious. I am going crazy all alone. I expected you the day before yesterday, and yesterday, and now I am writing to find out where you are. I wanted to come myself, but knew you would not like it. Send me an answer, so that I may know what to do.'

The child ill, but she had thought of coming herself! Their daughter ill, and this angry tone!

Vronsky thought how much of a contrast there was between the happy celebrations at the elections, and the dark, heavy love to which he must return. But he would have to go, and by the first train that night he set off for home.

Anna had been determined, when Vronsky left for the elections, not to argue or cause him any problems. But his cold tone of voice when he came to tell her he was going had wounded her.

Later, when she was alone, she thought to herself, 'He has the right to go when and where he chooses. Not simply to go away, but to leave me. He has all the rights, while I have none. But what did he do? Looked at me coldly and severely. Of course there was nothing definite, but it wasn't like that before. That look shows his love is beginning to cool.'

Anna was sure that Vronsky was losing interest in her, but there was nothing she could do. The only way to stop herself thinking about it was by keeping herself busy during the day and taking morphine at night. The thought that he might cease to love her was terrible. She realized that the only way to hold him was by obtaining a divorce, and made up her mind to agree the next time he asked her about it.

During Vronsky's absence, she filled her time with walks, visits to the hospital and reading. But on the sixth day, when he had still not returned, she could no longer stop thinking about what he was doing away from her. Then the little girl became ill and, towards the evening, she decided to send a letter to Vronsky by special messenger. The next morning, she received his note and regretted her own. The baby was getting better; what would he say when he discovered she was not dangerously ill? Then Anna felt happy again. He was coming; what did it matter if he was tired of her, as long as she could see him and know all his movements?

She was sitting by a lamp in the sitting room, reading and listening to the wind outside. At last she heard the sound of his carriage outside, and then his voice, and forgetting everything, ran joyfully down the stairs to greet him.

'Well, how is Ani?' he asked at once, sitting on a chair while a servant pulled off his boots.

'Oh, it's nothing. She's better.'

'Well, I'm very glad,' he said, looking coldly at her, at her hair and the dress which he knew she had put on for him. He liked and admired it all, but he had admired it so often!

The evening passed happily; he told her about the elections and Anna described cheerfully everything of interest that had happened at home.

But late at night she said, 'Confess that you were angry at getting my letter?'

'Yes,' he said. 'It was such a strange letter. First Ani ill, then you thought of coming yourself. You somehow refuse to realize there are duties . . .'

'Yes, like the duty of going to a concert and a ball . . .'

'Don't let's talk about it,' he said. 'Sometimes I have business which I can't avoid. Now, for example, I have to go to Moscow.'

'If you go to Moscow, I shall come too,' said Anna. 'I will not stay here alone. Either we must separate, or else live together all the time.'

'You know that is my one desire too. But for that . . .'

'I must get a divorce? I will write to him. I see I cannot go on like this . . . But I shall come with you to Moscow.'

'You make it sound like a threat when my greatest wish is never to be apart from you,' said Vronsky, smiling. But the look that flashed in his eyes as he spoke the tender words was not only cold – it was very angry. 'If you behave like this, it means disaster!' his glance told her.

Anna wrote to her husband asking him about a divorce, and towards the end of November she moved with Vronsky to Moscow. Expecting every day a reply from Karenin, and then the divorce, they set up house together like a married couple.

Chapter 13   Return to Moscow

The Levins had been in Moscow for over two months. The date had long passed on which Kitty should have had her baby, but she was still waiting. Levin, Dolly and her mother were impatient and anxious, but Kitty felt perfectly calm and happy.

She was surrounded by all the people she loved, and they were so good to her, and took such good care of her, that she could not desire a better life. She knew however that Levin did not feel comfortable in town and missed his life in the country.

He had nothing to do in Moscow; he did not like playing cards and did not belong to a club. She did not want him to go out drinking with the young men of Moscow, or into society without her. Sometimes he worked on a book he was writing, and went to the library to take notes and find references.

One evening Oblonsky invited Levin to his club, and Levin enjoyed the excellent dinner and friendly atmosphere very much. The conversation was about horse racing. There had been races that day, and a horse belonging to Vronsky had won first prize. Suddenly, Levin saw Vronsky come in.

'Very glad to meet you again,' Vronsky said to Levin. 'I looked for you again at the elections, but I was told you had gone.'

'Yes, I left the same day. We were just talking about your horse. Congratulations!' replied Levin.

Whether it was due to the influence of the atmosphere of the club, or the wine he had drunk, Levin chatted to Vronsky quite easily, without any feelings of dislike.

Oblonsky, who had had a lot to drink, said to Vronsky, 'This is a true friend of mine – almost my best friend. You also have become nearer and dearer to me. I want you to be friends.'

'Well, then, let's be friends,' said Vronsky in a good-natured way, holding out his hand. Levin took the hand and pressed it warmly.

'I am very, very glad,' he said.

'Waiter, another bottle of wine!' called Oblonsky. Then, turning to Vronsky, he said, 'What do you think – Levin has never met Anna. I am most eager to take him to see her.'

'She will be delighted to see you,' said Vronsky. 'I will not come home yet. A friend of mine, Yashvin, is playing cards, and I have to make sure he doesn't lose all his money.'

'Well, Levin?' said Oblonsky. 'Shall we visit Anna? She's a wonderful woman and I promised long ago to bring you.'

'Yes,' said Levin. 'I would like to meet her very much.'

They left the club and got into Oblonsky's carriage. For the first time, Levin began to wonder if it was right to go and see Anna. What would Kitty say? She would not like it. But Oblonsky gave him no time for thought.

'Anna is in a very difficult position,' he was saying. 'We are trying to make a deal with her husband about a divorce. He is willing, but there are difficulties in regard to the son, and the matter, which ought to have been settled long ago, has been dragging on for three months. As soon as she gets a divorce, she'll marry Vronsky and everything will be all right. But now, she doesn't go out and doesn't see anybody except Dolly.'

'She has a daughter, doesn't she, to take up her time?'

'Yes, she's bringing her daughter up splendidly, but she doesn't talk about the child much.'

The carriage stopped, and Oblonsky got out and rang the bell of a large house. A servant opened the door and Oblonsky walked into the hall, followed by Levin.

A lamp on the wall threw its light on the portrait of a woman. Levin could not take his eyes away from it; it was not a picture but a living, lovely woman with black curling hair, bare shoulders and arms, and a dreamy half-smile on her soft lips. It was more beautiful than a living woman could be.

'I'm delighted,' he heard a voice say – the voice of the woman in the portrait. Anna came out to greet him, and Levin saw in the soft light of the hall the woman of the portrait, in a dark dress of different shades of blue. She had the same perfection of beauty which the artist had caught.

'I'm delighted, delighted,' she repeated. 'I've known of you and liked you for a long time, both because of your friendship for Stiva and because of your wife ... I knew her for a very short time but she left on me the impression of a lovely flower. It's difficult to imagine that she'll soon be a mother!'

She spoke easily and slowly, looking from Levin to her brother. Levin immediately felt comfortable and happy with her, but could not stop looking at the portrait.

'It's wonderfully good, isn't it?' said Oblonsky.

'I never saw anything so perfect,' replied Levin.

They went into the study and started talking about art. Then they had tea, over which they continued the same sort of pleasant, interesting talk. Each of them felt there was not enough time to say all they wanted to.

All the time Levin was admiring Anna – her beauty, her intelligence, her cultured mind, the direct and sincere way in which she spoke. He was thinking of her and her inner life, trying to guess her feelings. And he was sorry for her and began to fear that Vronsky did not fully understand her. When Oblonsky got up to go, Levin was sorry to leave.

'Goodbye,' said Anna, holding his hand and glancing into his face with a look that drew him to her. 'I'm so glad we're now friends. Tell your wife that I have the same feelings for her as before, and I hope she can forgive me my position.'

'What a wonderful, sweet woman!' thought Levin, as he and Oblonsky stepped out into the frosty air.

'What did I tell you?' said Oblonsky, who saw that Anna had completely charmed Levin.

'Yes, she's really wonderful,' said Levin. 'She's clever and she has a very warm heart. I feel very sorry for her.'

Still thinking of Anna and the conversation they had had, and recalling all her expressions, Levin reached home. He found Kitty sad and depressed. Her mother and Dolly had come to dinner with her, but afterwards they had waited and waited for him. The evening had seemed long, and after her mother and sister had gone Kitty had been left alone.

'Well, what have you been doing?' she asked.

'I met Vronsky at the club. I was really very glad to meet him. I felt quite comfortable and natural with him. And afterwards, Stiva begged me to go and see Anna.'

Kitty's eyes opened wide and flashed at the mention of Anna. Seeing this, Levin turned red. He knew now that he ought not to have gone.

'I'm sure you won't be angry with me for going. She is very charming, and nice – and very much to be pitied,' he said.

He told Kitty about his visit and then went to undress. When he came back, he found Kitty still sitting in the same armchair. She looked at him and burst into tears.

'What is it? What's the matter?' he asked.

'You've fallen in love with that hateful woman,' she said. 'I saw it in your eyes. We must go away, we must go away tomorrow.'

It was a long time before Levin could calm his wife. At last, he succeeded in calming her only by admitting that the wine he had drunk had been too much for him, and by promising that he would avoid Anna in the future.

But a few hours later, Kitty woke and realized that her baby was on its way, and Levin was sent hurriedly for the doctor. The next twenty-four hours were a very emotional time for Levin, as he listened to his wife's cries of pain, unable to do anything to help her. But everything was fine, and Kitty had a healthy baby boy. Levin was filled with a deep joy. He was a father.

◆

When Levin and Oblonsky left Anna, she did not sit down but walked up and down the room. She had liked Levin and knew that he liked her, but as soon as he left, she forgot him.

She had one thought only. 'Why, when other men like me – why is *he* so cold to me? No, not cold exactly – I am sure he still loves me – but something has come between us.

'He ought to realize how miserable my life is here in Moscow – if it can be called life. I don't live – waiting for a solution that never comes. Still no answer! And I can't write again, I can't do anything, begin anything, change anything! I just have to wait and invent ways of passing the time, so I don't have to think – that's why I take morphine.'

She heard Vronsky's ring at the front door and quickly sat down by the lamp and opened a book, trying to appear calm.

'Well, you've not been lonely?' he asked her cheerfully.

'No. Stiva and Levin were here. They only left a short time ago. How did Yashvin get on playing cards?'

'He won a lot of money at first, but then he went back, and now he's losing.'

'Then what reason was there for you to stay?' she asked, with a cold expression on her face. 'You told Stiva you were staying only for the purpose of bringing Yashvin away. And now you've abandoned him!'

Vronsky frowned as he replied, 'I didn't give Stiva any message for you. But the chief point is, I stayed because I wanted to. Anna, Anna, why do you do this?' he said, bending towards her and putting his hand out, but she did not take it.

'Of course you wanted to stay, and you stayed! You always do what you want. When I feel as I do now, that you dislike me –

yes, dislike me – if you knew what this means for me! If you knew how near disaster I am at such moments, how afraid I am – afraid of myself!' And she turned away to hide her tears.

'But what is all this about?' he asked. 'What have I done? I am ready to do anything to make you happy.'

'It's nothing, it's nothing!' she said. 'I don't know what makes me like this – whether it's the lonely life, or my nerves. But let's say no more about it. Tell me about the races.'

Anna had won a victory over him. He began telling her about the races, but his voice and eyes grew colder and colder. She recalled her own words – 'how near disaster I am, how afraid of myself' – and realized that she could not use this weapon again. She felt that, joined with their love, there was an evil spirit which she could not remove from his heart or hers.

◆

Oblonsky's affairs were in a bad way. He had no money and the whole problem, in his view, was that his salary was too low. All his friends were earning more than he was, and doing less work.

He had heard of a very good position in Petersburg, and went there to pay a personal visit to some people whom he was hoping would use their influence to help him. One of these was Karenin, whom he also wanted to talk to about Anna's divorce.

Karenin was unwilling to help Oblonsky obtain a better position and advised him to go and see someone else. Oblonsky was very disappointed, but then he remembered that he still had to ask Karenin about Anna.

At the mention of Anna's name, Karenin's face changed completely, and he looked tired and lifeless.

'What exactly do you want of me?' he asked.

'A decision. If you had seen her all this winter, you would feel great pity for her. Her position is awful, awful!'

'I thought she had everything she wanted,' said Karenin.

'Please, Alexei. You know what she is wanting and hoping for – a divorce.'

'But I understood she did not want a divorce, if I insist on keeping the boy. The matter is closed.'

'No,' said Oblonsky. 'The matter is not closed. When you and Anna separated, you were ready to give her everything – her freedom, a divorce. She appreciated it so much, knowing how she had wronged you, but at that time she could not consider everything. But now she cannot bear her situation. I will arrange it all for you. You did promise, you remember.'

'That promise was given earlier,' replied Karenin. 'And I thought the question of my son had settled the matter. Also I, as a religious man, cannot go against the teaching of Christianity in such a serious matter.'

'But in Christian societies, and in ours too, divorce is allowed,' Oblonsky reminded him.

'I beg you,' began Karenin, rising suddenly to his feet, pale and trembling, 'I beg you to drop . . . to drop this subject! I refuse to divorce my wife!'

Chapter 14 Despair

It was summer again, and Vronsky and Anna were still in Moscow. It was very hot, but instead of going to Vronsky's country estate, they stayed in town.

Anna was sure now that Vronsky's love for her was declining. Vronsky was regretting that, because of Anna, he had placed himself in a difficult position. Neither spoke openly to the other about their feelings, but each thought the other was in the wrong and took every opportunity to prove it.

Anna was also very jealous, and felt sure that Vronsky had transferred the love which should have been concentrated on her to another woman. This was her worst fear, particularly since he had once told her, without thinking, that his mother wanted him to marry the pretty young Princess Sorokina, who was staying with her at her country house near Moscow.

Anna blamed Vronsky for everything she had to bear – her loneliness, her long wait in Moscow, Karenin's indecision. If he had loved her, he would have rescued her from the miserable position she was in. It was his fault, too, that they were living in Moscow instead of in the country. And it was also his fault that she was separated from her son forever.

One evening, Anna was waiting for Vronsky to return from a dinner party. They had quarrelled the day before and he had been away from home for the whole day. Anna was feeling miserable and lonely and had decided that she would forgive him everything so that they could be friends again.

At ten o'clock Vronsky came in.

'Well, did you have a good time?' she asked.

'The same as usual,' he replied, seeing at once that she was in one of her good moods.

'Alexei,' she said. 'I went out for a drive, and it was so lovely I wanted to be in the country. Why should we go on waiting here for the divorce? We can wait just as well in the country.'

'Yes, I agree,' he said. 'My one wish is to get away. When do you think of going?'

'We could be ready to go the day after tomorrow.'

'Yes – oh no, wait a moment – the day after tomorrow is Sunday and I have to go and see my mother,' said Vronsky, embarrassed because he felt Anna's eyes fixed on him.

His embarrassment confirmed Anna's suspicions. At once she began to think about the young Princess Sorokina.

'You could go there tomorrow,' she said.

'No. I'm going to my mother's on business – to take her some money. It won't be ready by tomorrow.'

'Well, then, we won't go to the country at all!' said Anna.

'Why not? We can go in a few days.'

'No,' said Anna. 'If you loved me, you would want to go immediately. And if you don't love me any more, it would be better and more honest to say so!'

She turned towards the door, but Vronsky took her hand.

'Wait! I don't understand,' he said. 'What is this all about? I said we must postpone our departure for a few days, and you accuse me of not loving you any more.'

Without looking round, Anna went slowly up to her room.

'He hates me, that is clear,' she thought. 'He's in love with another woman, and that is even clearer. I want love, but it has gone. It's all over, and I must end it. But how?'

Thoughts passed through her mind – what was Vronsky doing now, alone in his study; was this their final quarrel; what would Karenin think; what would all her old Petersburg friends say about her? But there was one thought at the back of her mind, which she knew was the only important one. Thinking of Karenin again, she recalled the time of her illness. 'Why didn't I die then?' she thought. 'Yes, death! That would solve everything.

'If I die, the shame and disgrace I have brought on my husband and Seriozha will all be wiped out,' she thought. 'And if I die, *he too* will be sorry.' A smile of self-pity settled on her lips as she sat in her chair, pulling off and on her rings and imagining all Vronsky's different feelings after she was dead.

The next morning, as they were sitting at breakfast, a telegram came for Vronsky from Petersburg. Anna, noticing that he was trying to hide something from her, asked him who it was from.

He hesitated and said, 'From Stiva.'

'Why didn't you want to show it to me?'

'All right,' he said unwillingly. 'Read it for yourself.'

Anna took the telegram with shaking fingers and read, *'Have seen Karenin, but little hope of divorce.'*

'There was no need to hide this from me,' Anna said. 'I'm not upset by this news. A divorce doesn't interest me. Why does it interest you so much?'

'Because I like things to be definite,' he replied. 'And I think that the reason you get angry so easily is because of the uncertainty of your position.'

'But my position is very certain. I am completely in your power. You are the one whose position is uncertain . . .'

'Anna, if you imagine that I want to be free . . .'

'I really do not care what your mother thinks and whom she wants to marry you to.'

'But we are not talking about that!'

'Yes, we are. And let me tell you, I do not care about a heartless woman, whether she is old or not, and I do not want to have anything to do with her!'

'Anna, please do not speak about my mother with so little respect!' Vronsky said with a cold and angry expression.

Anna spent all day in her room. As she poured out her usual morphine, again the idea of death presented itself as the only solution to her problems. Nothing mattered to her now – whether they went to the country, whether she got a divorce or not. The only thing that mattered was to punish Vronsky.

That night she had the same horrible dream which she had had several times since she had known Vronsky. A little old peasant man with a dirty beard was bending over her, muttering strange things in French and doing something terrible to her with a piece of iron. She awoke in a cold sweat.

When she got up, she remembered the quarrel of the previous day. Learning that Vronsky was in his study, she started to go there to tell him that she was ready to leave for the country whenever he wanted to go.

But then she heard a carriage stop at the front door and, looking out of the window, saw a pretty young girl lean out. Anna saw Vronsky run out of the house and down the steps to the carriage. The young girl handed him a packet. Vronsky said something to her and she smiled. The carriage drove off.

The feelings of the previous day returned to bring fresh pain to Anna's aching heart. She could not understand how she could have humiliated herself to remain one more day with Vronsky. She went to his study to tell him she had decided to leave.

'That was the Princess Sorokina,' he said. 'She brought me some documents from my mother, which I need so that I can obtain the money for her.'

Anna stood silently in the middle of the room and stared at him with a tragic look on her face. Then she went to the door.

'We are definitely going tomorrow, aren't we?' he asked.

'You are, but not I,' she said, turning round to him.

'Anna, we can't go on like this . . .'

'You . . . you will be sorry for this,' she said, and went out.

He saw the despair in her eyes and jumped up, meaning to run after her. But then he changed his mind and sat down again, frowning. 'I've tried everything,' he thought. 'The only thing left now is to leave her alone.'

Anna heard his steps in the hall, then the sound of the carriage. She went to the window and saw him get in and say something to the coachman. Then, without a glance at the window, he settled himself in the carriage and left.

'He's gone! It's all over!' she said to herself, and an icy horror seized her heart. 'No, no, it cannot be!'

She crossed the room and rang for a servant.

'Where has Count Vronsky gone?' she asked.

'To the railway station,' replied the servant. 'He is going to catch a train to Obiralovka.'

Obiralovka was the area where Vronsky's mother had her country house. Anna sat down and hurriedly wrote a note.

It's all my fault. Come back home. We must talk about things. For God's sake come back! I am very frightened.

The servant took the note and, afraid of being alone, Anna

went to the nursery. But when she saw the little girl, her first thought was, 'This is not right – this is not he! Where are his blue eyes? Where is his sweet, shy smile?' In the confusion of her thoughts, she had expected to find Seriozha. She sat down and started playing with the baby, but the child's expressions reminded her so much of Vronsky that she had to leave.

She looked at the clock. Twelve minutes had passed. 'Now he must have received my note and be on his way back,' she thought. 'I mustn't let him see that I've been crying. I'll go and wash my eyes. And what about my hair – have I done it or not?' She had, but she could not remember doing it.

Glancing out of the window she saw his carriage return, but nobody came upstairs. She went down and met the servant she had sent after him and who had come back in the carriage.

'I didn't catch Count Vronsky. The train had already left,' he said, and handed her back her note.

'Well, take the note to Countess Vronsky's country house, and bring back an answer at once,' she told the man. Then she wrote out a telegram as well, in the hope that it would reach Vronsky more quickly than the note.

'I absolutely must talk to you; come at once.'

Having given the telegram to the man, she went upstairs to dress. Her maid looked at her with sympathetic eyes.

'Don't be so upset, madam,' she said. 'Why don't you go out? A change will do you good.'

'Yes, I will go out,' thought Anna, listening to the beating of her heart. 'I must do something, get away from this house.'

Anna went to see Dolly, but the visit did not go well; it was clear that Anna was not interested in anything that Dolly talked about. When she arrived home, a servant met her in the hall and handed her a telegram.

'I cannot return before ten. Vronsky.'

Anna did not consider that Vronsky's telegram had been in reply to her own telegram and that he had not yet received the note that the servant was taking to him. She imagined him calmly chatting with his mother and Princess Sorokina, and being glad about her sufferings. 'I must go there at once to talk to him,' she thought. She looked at the railway timetable in the daily paper. There was an evening train at two minutes past eight. 'Yes, I shall be in time.'

She packed a travelling bag with the things she might need for a few days. She knew she would never return. Dinner was on the table, but the whole idea of food disgusted her. She ordered the carriage and went out. Her maid came out with her things, and put them in the carriage; she got in, and the coachman drove off.

The people Anna passed in the streets all seemed to have empty, meaningless lives. She thought about Vronsky and for the first time saw their affair in a clear new light.

'What did he look for in me?' she thought. 'Not love, but only pride in his success with me. He has taken from me everything he could, and now I am of no more use to him.

'My love is becoming more and more passionate and selfish, while his is dying, and that is why we are growing apart. He is everything to me, and I want him to give himself more and more entirely to me, but he wants to go farther and farther away from me. He has ceased to love me, and where love ends, hate begins.

'If I get divorced and become his wife, it will not change anything – there will be no new feeling. And what about Seriozha? Seriozha! I thought too that I loved him, but I have lived here without him and did not complain as long as the other love satisfied me.'

They arrived at the station, and the coachman asked, 'Shall I buy a ticket to Obiralovka?'

She had completely forgotten where she was going and could not understand his question, but then she remembered.

'Yes,' she said, handing him her purse; and, hanging her little red bag on her arm, she got out of the carriage.

She looked at all the people waiting for the train, and did not like any of them. She thought of how she would arrive at Obiralovka and send Vronsky a note from the station there. She thought of how she loved and hated him, and hope and despair in turn filled her wildly beating heart.

Anna got into a carriage of the train, feeling that the other passengers were staring at her in a strange and unpleasant way. Suddenly, as she looked out of the window, waiting for the train to start, she saw a dirty old peasant bending down to the carriage wheels. 'There's something familiar about that old peasant,' thought Anna, and then she remembered her dream. Trembling with fear, she went to the door of the carriage, but a man and his wife were coming in and she could not get out.

The train started, and the wheels made a slight ringing sound as they moved along. The bright evening sun shone through the window. When the train stopped at Obiralovka, she got out with a crowd of other passengers. She stopped a guard and asked him if there was not a coachman anywhere with a note from Count Vronsky.

'Yes, Count Vronsky's coachman was here just now, to meet Princess Sorokina. I think he is still here.'

A few minutes later, the coachman came up and handed her a note. Vronsky had written in a careless hand,

'Sorry your note did not catch me. I shall be back at ten.'

'Yes, this is what I expected!' said Anna to herself. She walked down the platform. 'Oh, God, where shall I go?' she thought, walking further and further down the platform and stopping at the end. She walked to the edge. A goods train was approaching and the platform began to shake.

In a flash she remembered the man who had been run down by the train the day she first met Vronsky, and she knew what she had to do. Quickly and lightly she walked down the steps from the platform to the tracks, and stopped close to the passing train. She looked at the tall iron wheels of the first truck slowly moving up, and tried to measure the point midway between the front and back wheels and the exact moment when it would be opposite her.

'There,' she said to herself. 'There, in the middle, and I shall punish him and escape from them all and from myself.'

It was too late; the first truck had passed. But the second truck was approaching, and exactly at the moment when the space between the wheels came level with her, she dropped on her hands under the truck and with a light movement sank on to her knees. At that same moment she was filled with horror at what she was doing. 'Where am I? What am I doing? Why?'

She tried to get up again and throw herself back, but something huge struck her on the head and dragged her down on her back. 'God forgive me everything!' she whispered, feeling the impossibility of struggling.

A little peasant muttering something to himself was working at the rails. And the light by which she had been seeing all the problems, deceit, sorrow and evil shone brightly, making clear for her everything which had been in darkness, then grew weak and went out forever.

Chapter 15   The Way Forward

Nearly two months had passed, but the hot summer was only half over. A group of soldiers were at the railway station, on their way to fight in the Serbian war against the Turks. They were accompanied by a happy and excited crowd, who had come to the station to give them flowers and wish them good luck. A thousand soldiers had already left Russia to take part in the war, and the news from the war zone was good; for the past three days the Turkish army had been losing.

Oblonsky was at the station, but he was not going on the train. He had come to say goodbye to a friend of his, one of the soldiers who was leaving.

'What a pity you are going away,' said Oblonsky. 'We are having such a fine dinner party tomorrow.'

'People are saying that Vronsky is on the train,' said his friend. 'His mother is with him. He's going as a volunteer, and taking a whole group of soldiers with him at his own expense.'

'Really?' replied Oblonsky. 'Then I must go and say goodbye to him.' A look of grief passed over his face, but a moment later, when he saw Vronsky on the platform walking towards the train, he had quite forgotten his sister's death, and saw Vronsky only as a hero and an old friend.

Vronsky, in a long overcoat and black hat, was walking with his mother on his arm. Oblonsky started to talk to him in an animated way, but Vronsky frowned and looked straight in front of him as if he did not hear. His face, aged and full of suffering, looked like stone. He reached the train and let his mother go in front of him before silently disappearing into one of the carriages.

The train set off. It stopped a few hours later at the main town of the province, and the soldiers walked up and down the platform. Vronsky's mother was at the window of her carriage. She saw a young officer she knew on the platform and waved to him. The man had known Vronsky in his former army days.

'I'm going as far as Kursk with my son,' she said.

'Really?' replied the young officer. 'What a fine thing he's doing!' he added, seeing that Vronsky was not in the carriage.

'Yes,' she said. 'After what happened, what else can he do? It's the best thing for him in the circumstances. You can't think what I've suffered. But won't you come in?'

The young officer saw that she wanted to talk, and entered the carriage and took a seat beside her.

'You can't imagine!' she went on. 'For six weeks he never said a word to anyone, and would not touch food except when I begged him. And we dared not leave him alone for a single minute – we were afraid he would kill himself.

'The evening it happened was terrible. We were at my country house. We had no idea she was at the station. I was just going to bed when my servant brought a note that a lady had thrown herself under a train. I knew at once it was she. My first words were, "Don't tell him!" but he had already heard. His coachman was there and saw it all.

'Without a word, he rushed to the station. I don't know what happened there, but they brought him back like a dead man. Then he went crazy. It was a terrible time. Can you understand these desperate passions? She was a bad woman. She brought ruin to herself and two fine men – her husband and my unfortunate son.'

'And how about her husband?' asked the young officer.

'He took the little girl. Alexei was ready to consent to anything at first, but now he is very upset that he gave up his own daughter to another man. Karenin came to the funeral, but we did all we could to prevent him from meeting Alexei. For her husband it is easier – she had set him free. But my poor son had given up everything – his career, me – and even then she had no mercy on him. No, her death was the death of a bad woman, a woman without religion. God forgive me, but I can't help hating her memory when I look at the ruin of my son.'

'But how is he now?'

'This Serbian war is like a gift from God for him. I'm an old woman, and I don't understand the rights and wrongs of it, but for him it came at the right time. Of course, as his mother, I feel terrible that he is going. But Yashvin, a friend of his, had lost all his money and was going as a volunteer, and persuaded my son to go too. Now it's the only thing that interests him. He is so miserable, and on top of everything else he has toothache. He will be very glad to see you. Please go and talk to him.'

Vronsky, in a long overcoat, his hat pulled down low and his hands in his pockets, was walking up and down the platform like an animal in a cage. The young officer approached him, and Vronsky stopped, recognized him and came forward.

'Perhaps you would prefer not to see me,' said the young officer, 'but I thought I might be able to help you in some way.'

'Thank you, but I don't need anything,' replied Vronsky. 'I'm going to this war in the hope that I will die. My life is not simply useless but also hateful to me. Anyone can have it.'

'You will come back as a new man,' said the young officer. 'You're doing a great thing. Saving one's fellow-men from suffering is an aim worth dying for – and living for, too. May God give you success – and peace,' he added, holding out his hand.

Vronsky pressed it warmly, but could hardly speak because of the terrible pain in his tooth. He was silent, staring at the wheels of an approaching goods truck that was moving smoothly over the rails. And at once a different feeling, a terrible inner pain, made him forget his toothache. The sight of the truck and the rails made him recall *her* – as much as was left of her when he had rushed like a madman into the railway station and seen her mangled body, still warm with recent life, stretched out on a table. The head, which had escaped hurt, was thrown back, and the lovely face with its half-open red lips had frozen into a strange expression – pitiful on the lips and horrible in the fixed open eyes. It was as if she was repeating that terrible threat – that he would be sorry – that she had made during their last quarrel. He would never forget it.

And he tried to remember her as she was when he met her the first time – also at a railway station – mysterious, beautiful and loving, and not cruel and full of thoughts of revenge as he remembered her at the end. He tried to recall his best moments with her, but those moments were poisoned for ever. He ceased to feel the pain in his tooth, and started to cry.

◆

Levin and Kitty were back home in the country with their baby, Mitya. Kitty, busy in her role as a mother, was very calm and happy, but Levin could not find peace of mind. Since his brother's death, he had been thinking deeply about life and death and had experienced some terrible moments of uncertainty. His life seemed to have no meaning at all when he started to think about it. He looked for an answer in everything to his questions: 'What am I? Where am I? And why am I here?'

On his return to the country at the beginning of June, he started to work hard again on the farm. The management of his estate, the peasants, his wife and the baby all kept him very busy. But still he could not find happiness or peace. He did not believe in God, so could find no answers in religion.

He had hoped that his feelings for Mitya would give him some answers, but this did not happen. He began to be afraid he had no real feelings for his baby son.

One afternoon, Kitty took Mitya to the woods near the house. While she was there, the weather changed; the sky turned black, and a great storm began to blow up. When Levin learned from the servants that Kitty had gone out, he rushed after her at once.

He knew that her favourite place was an open space with a large oak tree, and that she loved sitting under this tree. As he approached it, he thought he saw something white underneath it. Suddenly, there was a great flash of lightning and the whole earth seemed on fire. This was followed by a loud roar of thunder. Levin, blinded by the flash of light, shut his eyes, but when he opened them again he saw to his horror that the oak tree had been struck by lightning. Moments later, it crashed to the ground.

'Oh God! Oh God! Not on them!' he thought. He ran to the place where he thought he had seen Kitty, but she was not there. Then he heard someone calling his name and saw her at the other end of the open space, holding Mitya and smiling.

'Alive? Safe? Thank God!' he muttered.

For the whole of the rest of the day, Levin's heart was full of happiness. Later, he went to see the baby in the nursery where Kitty was giving him his bath. Hearing her husband's step, she turned round and smiled, as she supported the head of the baby with one hand and washed him with the other.

'Look, look!' she said excitedly. 'He knows us!'

It was true. Mitya had begun to show that he recognized both Kitty and Levin. When they leaned over him, his face lit up with a smile. Levin was surprised and delighted. Kitty took Mitya out of his bath, dried him and wrapped him in a towel.

'I'm glad you're beginning to be fond of him,' she said to her husband. 'You said you had no feeling for him, and it was beginning to worry me.'

'I only meant that I was disappointed.'

'What? Disappointed in him?'

'No. In my own feeling for him. But now a new feeling has awakened in me. I never knew until today, after my terror during the storm, how much I loved him.'

Kitty's smile was bright and warm.

'Were you very frightened?' she asked. 'I was, too. But now everything is all right. What a happy day we have had.'

When he had left the nursery and was alone again, Levin went outside. It had grown quite dark and to the south, where he was looking, the sky was clear and there were bright stars.

'The new feeling that I have now has not changed me; I shall still go on as before. But every minute of my life now, my whole life, is no longer meaningless as it was previously, but has a positive goodness of meaning which I have the power to give it.'

ACTIVITIES

Chapters 1–3

Before you read

1 Discuss these questions with another student.
   a This story has a very famous opening line: 'All happy families are alike, but an unhappy family is unhappy in its own way.' What does the writer mean? Do you agree with his statement? Why (not)?
   b What kind of activity might have been scandalous in the nineteenth century but would be more acceptable in many societies now?
   c Describe a recent public scandal that you have heard about. Why were people shocked? Were they right to be shocked? Were they right to be informed? Why (not)?

2 Read the Introduction to this book, and answer these questions.
   a When, and in which country, does the story take place?
   b What was Tolstoy's opinion of 'high society'?
   c How is Anna's relationship with Vronsky different from Kitty's with Levin?

3 Look at the Word List at the back of the book. Find words for
   a individual people
   b groups of people
   c feelings
   d causes of strong negative feelings

While you read

4 Who is being described?
   a He is in disgrace with his wife.   ....
   b He dislikes town life.   ....
   c She does not like Levin.   ....
   d She rejects a marriage proposal.   ....
   e His brother suffers from consumption.   ....
   f He helps a widow.   ....
   g She forgives her husband.   ....

h He follows Anna to Petersburg. ....

i She becomes pregnant. ....

j He falls off a horse. ....

After you read

5 Discuss who these words best describe. Which actions or events are being referred to?

a kind but guilty

b badly-behaved but popular

c angry but forgiving

d beautiful but afraid

e sensitive and sad

f generous and determined

6 How do these people feel, and why?

a Oblonsky, when he wakes up on the sofa.

b Levin, when he leaves the Skating Gardens.

c Levin, after his meal with Oblonsky in the grand Moscow restaurant.

d Levin, when he leaves the Shcherbatsky's house.

e Kitty and Anna, after the grand ball.

f Anna, after she sits down in the carriage outside Moscow station.

g Anna and Vronsky, after they arrive at Petersburg station.

h Vronsky's mother, when she hears of her son's relationship with Anna.

i Vronsky, when he learns that Anna is pregnant.

j Karenin, after the horse race.

7 Work with another student. Have this conversation between Kitty's parents after the grand ball.

Student A: You are Prince Shcherbatsky. You would prefer your daughter to marry Levin. Say why.

Student B: You are Princess Shcherbatskaya. You would prefer your daughter to marry Vronsky. Say why.

8 Is Anna wise to tell her husband about her love for Vronsky? Why (not)? Discuss your ideas.

Chapters 4 – 6

Before you read

9 What would you do now if you were Karenin? Why?

While you read

10 Are these sentences true (T) or false (F)?

    a While Levin works on his country estate, Kitty
        travels abroad with her parents.   .....

    b Levin helps solve Dolly's problems
        in the country house.   .....

    c Dolly tells Levin that her sister loves him.   .....

    d Levin briefly considers marrying a peasant girl.   .....

    e Karenin challenges Vronsky to a duel.   .....

    f Anna feels guilty about hurting her husband.   .....

    g Vronsky is pleased with Anna for telling her
        husband the truth.   .....

    h Levin visits Dolly while Kitty is with her.   .....

    i Nikolai is recovering from his illness.   .....

After you read

11 Who says, writes or thinks these words? Why?

    a 'If you only knew how you are hurting me!'

    b 'This is the only course of action suited to my religious
        principles.'

    c 'It's a torture for me and I can't live with it.'

    d 'It's difficult to love a woman and do anything.'

    e 'Things can't go on as he supposes.'

    f 'I think that is not too much to ask.'

    g 'I hope you will bring it over yourself.'

    h 'The important thing is to have one's health.'

12 'These were the only sincere words that had passed between
them.' Discuss these questions.

    a Whose words have been insincere? Why? Who is talking to?

    b What does he finally say that is meaningful? What do his words
        mean?

    c How do the two of them really feel about each other?

13 Work with another student. Have these conversations.

   a a conversation between Karenin and a colleague.

   Student A: Criticize Karenin's behaviour (in relation to Anna). What should he have done or not done? What advice would you give him for the future?

   Student B: You are Karenin. Defend your actions.

   b similar conversations between each of these people and a friend:

   Anna   Levin   Vronsky

Chapters 7–9

Before you read

14 What do you think will happen when these people meet?

   a Karenin and Vronsky

   b Levin and Kitty

   c Kitty and Nikolai

While you read

15 Write in the missing names.

   a .... and .... have the same dream.

   b .... shows a lawyer ....'s letters to ....

   c At the dinner party, ... has a serious conversation with ....

   d .... and .... write messages to each other on a card-table.

   e .... and .... shake hands at ....'s bedside.

   f .... tries to kill himself.

   g .... persuades .... to give .... a divorce.

   h .... and .... go to Italy, while .... and .... get married.

   i .... is kind to .... before he dies.

   j .... offers to help .... to look after ....

After you read

16 Think back to your answers to Activity 14. Were your predictions correct?

17 Which of these adjectives describe Anna in this part of the story? Why?

jealous frightened regretful bored happy embarrassed
angry hopeful amused

18 Discuss these questions with another student. What do you think?

    a What are the final letters that Levin writes for Kitty at the card-table?

    b Who do you feel most sorry for in this part of the story? Why?

19 'There, wetting the frightened boy's cheeks with her tears, she told him that his father was a saint and his mother was dead.' How sympathetic are you to the Countess and her behaviour? What do you think her motives are?

Chapters 10–12

Before you read

20 Do you think it is a wise decision for Anna to return to Petersburg? What problems might she face there?

While you read

21 Number these events in the correct order, 1–10.

    a Anna and Vronsky go to Moscow.   .....

    b Vronsky asks Dolly for help.   .....

    c Anna sees her son.   .....

    d Levin and Kitty move to Moscow.   .....

    e The Countess Lydia Ivanovna and Anna exchange letters.   .....

    f Dolly visits Anna.   .....

    g Anna and Vronsky go to the country.   .....

    h Anna meets Prince Yashvin.   .....

    i Vronsky meets Levin again.   .....

    j Anna is publicly humiliated.   .....

After you read

22 Match the first parts of the sentences with the correct endings.

    a Soon after she arrives in Petersburg, Anna feels
       hurt and angry because she …   .....

    b Anna does not discuss her feelings with Vronsky
       because he …   .....

    c Seriozha is confused because his mother …   .....

    d Vronsky does not want Anna to go to the opera
       because he …   .....

    e Anna is upset after the opera because she …   .....

    f Dolly changes her mind about Vronsky because she …   .....

    g Vronsky wants Anna to divorce Karenin because he …   .....

    h Dolly is shocked because Anna …   .....

    i Vronsky goes to Kashin because he …

    j Anna takes morphine because she …

    1) does not want to have more children.

    2) would not understand them.

    3) wants to have legal rights to his children.

    4) wants to help a friend.

    5) does not want to cause a lot of gossip.

    6) cannot sleep.

    7) says that she has been wicked.

    8) receives a cruel and unexpected letter.

    9) has seen his work on a new hospital.

    10) has been publicly humiliated.

23 Work with another student. Have this conversation between two people who witnessed the events at the opera.

    Student A: You are shocked by Anna's behaviour. Explain why.

    Student B: You feel sorry for Anna. Explain why.

24 Discuss these questions with another student.

    a Why don't Levin and Kitty want to meet Vronsky?

    b How does Vronsky prevent himself from being bored?

    c How does Dolly feel after her visit to Anna and Vronsky? Why?

    d Is Anna a good mother? Why (not)?

    e How have Anna's and Vronsky's feelings about each other changed?

Chapters 13–15

Before you read

25 Do you think that *Anna Karenina* going to have a happy ending? Why (not)?

26 Whose words do you think these will be?

    a 'What do you think – Levin has never met Anna. I am most eager to take him to see her.'

    b 'Tell your wife that I have the same feelings for her as before, and I hope she can forgive me my position.'

    c 'You were drinking and drinking at the club, and then you went . . . to her, of all people.'

    d 'Of course you wanted to stay, and you stayed! You always do what you want.'

    e 'I, as a religious man, cannot go against the teaching of Christianity in such a serious matter.'

While you read

27 Circle the correct answer.

    a Levin *admires / distrusts* Anna.

    b Karenin refuses to *forgive / divorce* Anna.

    c Anna quarrels with Vronsky because he *won't leave immediately / is in love with another woman*.

    d Oblonsky's telegram from Petersburg upsets *Anna / Vronsky*.

    e When she arrives at the station, Anna feels *calm but angry / confused and unhappy*.

    f Anna is afraid because she *knows that she will not return to Moscow / sees an old peasant*.

    g Anna *dies in an accident / kills herself*.

    h Anna's daughter is being looked after by *Karenin / Vronsky*.

    i Vronsky volunteers for the army because he wants to *fight for his country / die*.

After you read

28 How are these important in this part of the story?
  a Oblonsky
  b Princess Sorokina
  c morphine
  d a peasant
  e a goods train
  f a war with Turkey
  g an oak tree
29 How do these people feel at the end of the story? Why?
  a Vronsky
  b Kitty and Levin
  c Karenin
  d Oblonsky and Dolly
30 Who or what is to blame for Anna's death? Could it have been avoided? Discuss your ideas with another student.

Writing

31 Imagine that you are a reporter working for a local newspaper. Write an account of Anna's death.
32 How did Levin's brother, Nikolai, a religious man from a wealthy family, become a wild, drunken man living with a prostitute? Write his story.
33 Imagine that you are Vronsky (Chapter 3). You know that Kitty is ill and depressed after your rejection of her at the ball. Write a letter to her from Petersburg, apologizing for your behaviour and explaining as gently as you can why you have gone to Petersburg.
34 Imagine that you are Vronsky (Chapter 8). Write a letter to Anna, explaining why you are going to kill yourself.
35 Imagine that you are Vronsky (Chapter 11). Write an article for your local newspaper, describing the new hospital that you are building for the peasants and why you are building it.

36 'Anna is a selfish and immoral woman who deserves her final punishment.' Do you agree with this statement? Why (not)? Write an article expressing your views for your school or college magazine.

37 Choose one of these pairs of people and compare them. Which of the two do you prefer? Why?

    a Karenin and Vronsky

    b Levin and Oblonsky

    c Anna and Dolly

38 Write about the importance of the railway and trains in the story.

39 What do we learn from *Anna Karenina* about nineteenth-century Russian society? Would you like to have lived in that environment at that time? Why (not)?

40 What do you think happens to either Levin and Kitty or Dolly and Oblonsky over the next few years? Write their story.

Answers for the Activities in this book are available from the Pearson English Readers website. A free Activity Worksheet is also available from the website. Activity worksheets are part of the Pearson English Readers Teacher Support Programme, which also includes Progress tests and Graded Reader Guidelines. For more information, please visit: www.pearsonenglishreaders.com

WORD LIST

adultery (n) sex by a married man or woman with someone who is not their wife or husband

animated (adj) lively and interesting

ball (n) a large, formal social event at which people dance

cavalry (n) soldiers who fight while riding horses

chalk (n) soft white rock, used for writing or drawing

consent (n/v) permission to do something

consumption (n) a disease of the lungs which, in the past, caused a slow death

despair (n) a feeling of great unhappiness and no hope

disgrace (n) loss of respect for a person and often their family because that person has done something very bad

duel (n) a fight between two people with guns or swords

estate (n) a large area of land in the countryside, usually with one large house on it

humiliate (v) to make someone appear stupid or weak

maid (n) a female servant

mangled (adj) badly damaged, caused by crushing or twisting

mazurka (n) a Polish dance

mistress (n) the female lover of a married man

morphine (n) a powerful drug used for stopping pain

mutter (v) to speak in a low, quiet voice which is difficult to hear, especially when you are complaining about something

omen (n) a sign of what will happen in the future

passion (n) a very strong feeling, usually of love or of belief in something

portrait (n) a painting, drawing or photograph of someone

prostitute (n) someone who has sex to earn money

regiment (n) a large group of soldiers

saddle (n) a leather seat that you put on the back of an animal so you can ride it

scandal (n) a situation or event that people think is immoral or shocking

telegram (n) a message sent using electrical signals

terrace (n) a flat area next to a building, where you can sit

torture (n/v) extreme pain or unhappiness over a long period of time, for example as a punishment

velvet (n) cloth with a soft surface on one side, used for making clothes and curtains, for example

volunteer (n) someone who chooses to join the army